Understanding Fever and Body Temperature

"At a time of increasing challenges regarding the provision of a healthcare and concerns around the use of antibiotics to manage infection, this book is timely addition to the field. The book provides a varied approach to exploring the use of body temperature measurement, including an interesting historical underpinning which acts a helpful refresher to the subject area. The integration of physiological and immunological knowledge offers a fresh perspective on the subject area which will be of interest to a wide multi-professional international audience. The final chapter consolidates learning from each chapter through a series of scenarios and questions."

—Nicola Carey, Reader in Long Term Conditions in the School of Health Sciences and member of the Faculty of Health & Medical Sciences, *University of Surrey*

"*Understanding Fever and Body Temperature* is a well written book on the fascinating topic of fever. The authors approach the subject from many angles, an approach made possible by expertize in several different areas related to fever and the measurement of body temperature. As a result, the book will be useful for a wide range of readers including people interested in thermometry and those meeting febrile patients as part of their profession."

—David Engblom, Professor of Clinical and Experimental Medicine (IKE), *Linköping University, Sweden*

"*Understanding Fever and Body Temperature* is an interesting and exciting book and a cross-disciplinary compendium to all aspects of body temperature: History, measurements, basic thermal physiology and immunology, clinical evaluation of body temperature, etc. Also the book does away with traditional thinking and acting in particular as regards fevers. The special and peculiarity of the book is the pedagogical approach "problem-based-learning": Reflections at the end of every chapter, a lot of patient scenarios from clinical practice and many very important clinical implications. So the book will be of interest and importance to all professionals in Health-Care"

— Susanne Herzog, Specialist Nurse of Intensive Care, MScN, *University of Applied Sciences, Diakonie Bielefeld, Germany*

"A very interesting book! This book helped me understand and learn in-depth information about body temperature and fever. It has definitely helped me a lot during medical school".

—Andrew Toros, medical student at
Linköping University, Sweden

Ewa Grodzinsky • Märta Sund Levander
Editors

Understanding Fever and Body Temperature

A Cross-disciplinary Approach to Clinical Practice

palgrave
macmillan

Editors
Ewa Grodzinsky
Department of Pharmaceutic Research
Linköping University
Linköping, Sweden

Märta Sund Levander
Department of Nursing
Linköping University
Linköping, Sweden

ISBN 978-3-030-21885-0 ISBN 978-3-030-21886-7 (eBook)
https://doi.org/10.1007/978-3-030-21886-7

Cover illustration: Marina Lohrbach_shutterstock.com

This Palgrave Macmillan imprint is published by the registered company Springer Nature Switzerland AG
The registered company address is: Gewerbestrasse 11, 6330 Cham, Switzerland

Foreword

In our daily lives, our body temperature is constantly changing due to natural biorhythms, active processes such as exercise, or passive processes such as exposure to cold or warm environments. The body's thermoregulatory defense system, acting through both physiological and behavioral mechanisms, normally prevents such changes from becoming too great and causing harm. Although such changes in body temperature pose little danger to our health, it is interesting that human beings often use dramatic terms to describe them. 'I'm freezing' and 'I'm boiling hot' are common subjective phrases in English, and similar terms are found in most other languages. These qualitative overstatements presumably stem from the age-old awareness of the health risks not only of illness but of exposure to extremes of ambient temperature, even though in the past the reasons were poorly understood. An enormous leap forward in our understanding of the importance of a regulated body temperature came with the development of thermometry. By providing quantitative information on body temperature, thermometry has played a major role in our understanding of body temperature variability. The present volume revolves around thermometry, taking the reader on a journey from the past to the present. Yet, while the emphasis is on the clinical importance of obtaining accurate, quantitative measurements of body temperature, the reader is also introduced to the most recent thinking on their clinical interpretation, especially in relation to fever. These ideas have arisen in a cross-disciplinary collaboration, using evidence-based practice to integrate physiological and immunological knowledge. The editors, Ewa Grodzinsky and Märta Sund Levander, have collaborated closely with international experts in essays on a range of topics, including historical perspectives on temperature measurement, temperature measurement technology, the clinical evaluation of body temperature, and basic thermal physiology and immunology. The volume concludes with a number of patient scenarios that bring all these insights together. Although primarily a textbook that lends itself particularly well to a problem-based learning approach, *Understanding Fever and Body Temperature: A Cross-disciplinary Approach to Clinical Practice* will also be of interest to all health-care professionals.

University of Tromsø
Tromsø, Norway

James B. Mercer

The Arctic University of Norway
Harstad, Norway
March 2019

Contents

About the Authors[1]

Ewa Grodzinsky, Reg. BLS, Ph.D., is an associate professor and a senior research scientist and university lecturer at the Medical Faculty, Linköping University, Sweden. She teaches laboratory sciences at the undergraduate, specialist, and advanced levels. She has several years of clinical and research experience in development, metrology, and improvement in laboratory science. Her contribution to this book is in the area of immunology in a physiological and clinical perspective.

Märta Sund Levander, Reg. Nurse, Ph.D., is an associate professor, a senior research scientist and university lecturer at the Medical Faculty Linköping University, Sweden. She teaches nursing students at the undergraduate, specialist, and advanced levels. She has several years of clinical and research experience as a specialized nurse, especially in critical care, eldercare, infection control, and research and development. Her contribution to this book is in the area of history and the assessment and evaluation of body temperature and its clinical implications.

Contributing writer Rosita Christensen is a lecturer at the Karolinska Institute in Stockholm and teaches students at both the undergraduate and the specialist level within the subjects of physiology and anatomy. She is trained in physiology, with a focus on environmental physiology, at the

[1] Ewa Grodzinsky and Märta Sund Levander are the editors of this book. They have worked closely in writing the chapters, for which they are personally responsible, and with editing the chapters of their co-authors.

Karolinska Institute and is a specialist in naprapathy, with an M.Sc. in Health Care Pedagogics. She has several years of clinical experience as a chiropractor and in sports medicine, critical care, and eldercare. Her contribution to this book is within physiology and thermoregulation.

Contributing writer Francis E. Ring was Professor of Medical Imaging and Head of the Medical Imaging Research Unit at the University of South Wales in the UK. Ring unfortunately passed away before he could see this work published. He had over 50 years of research experience in the studies of human body temperature and was a pioneer within the field of thermography and biomedical engineering—especially thermal imaging. His contribution to this book is a historical review of techniques to measure body temperature and the development of thermometers.

Contributing writer Rob Simpson is a senior research scientist at the National Physical Laboratory (NPL), the UK's National Measurement Institute. He has a Ph.D. in infrared thermal metrology for medical applications from the University of Glamorgan. He currently leads thermal imaging metrology research at the NPL. His Ph.D. studies involved the development of new and novel reference standards for diagnostic medical thermal imaging. These reference sources were patented, licensed, and commercialized. His contribution to this book is to provide an understanding of how instruments are linked to the international measurement system (SI), and of what factors should be taken into account to ensure confidence in measurements, including measurement standards, traceability, calibration, and other factors.

List of Figures

CHAPTER 1

Introduction to Understanding Fever and Body Temperature

The year 1871 saw the publication of the magisterial work *Medical Thermometry and Human Temperature*. Based on exhaustive measurements of axillary temperature by the German physician Carl August Wunderlich (1815–1910), the book was the first to define normal body temperature as 37.0 °C (98.6 °F) and 38.0 °C (100 °F) as fever. However, at that time, the physiological mechanisms of thermoregulation were not known, there was little knowledge of immunology and microbiology, and the technology needed for accurate clinical thermometers was in its infancy. Also, Wunderlich's measurements were performed on patients, suggesting that a large number of them may have been febrile. In the late nineteenth century, the English physician Sir Thomas Clifford Allbutt introduced the shorter clinical rectal mercury thermometer, which was later followed by the oral mercury thermometer. It was not until the 1960s that digital devices were introduced together with new techniques for non-invasive measurement of body temperature. The most recently developed thermometers use infrared radiation to estimate body temperature.

Besides advances in the technical aspects of thermometers, there has been progress in the understanding of the physiological and immunological processes which influence body temperature. However, thermoregulation, in terms of the diurnal rhythm and the physiological mechanisms which maintain a stable and balanced internal environment, was not understood until the 1950s. The role of female hormones was not appreciated until the 1970s. By that time, immunology and the full complexity

E. Grodzinsky, M. Sund Levander (eds.), *Understanding Fever and Body Temperature*, https://doi.org/10.1007/978-3-030-21886-7_1

of the immune system—the body's defense mechanism for removing foreign agents and restoring tissue structure and physiological function—was beginning to be understood.

The effect of antipyretics on body temperature had been known for decades, as had the results of treatment with penicillin and sulfonamide, but antipyretic use in clinical practice did not become common until the 1970s. During the same decade there was a significant improvement in laboratory methods, making it possible to understand in more detail the effector mechanisms used to eliminate foreign agents and protect the body from destruction, particularly the role of various cells and cytokines. In the 1990s, quality assurance and patient safety were highlighted, and today they are permanent obligations within health care. Together with the demand for evidence-based decision-making, this now forms the basis for ensuring good care. However, even though there has been tremendous development, progress has advanced along two parallel lines (Fig. 1.1).

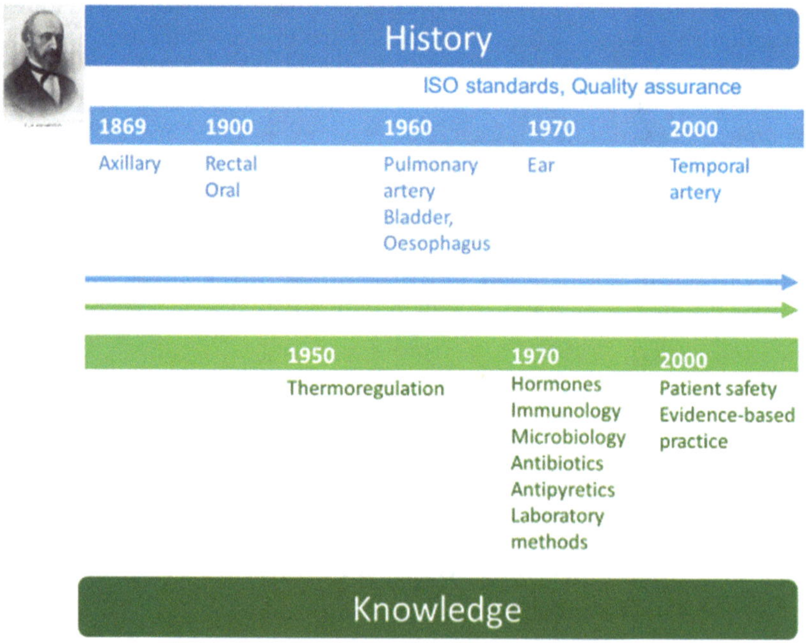

Fig. 1.1 The development of thermometry and physiological and immunological knowledge in relation to assessment of body temperature. (Copyright Grodzinsky, E & Sund Levander, M)

This parallel development has had great impact on current practices and perceptions about body temperature. The concept of fever influences clinical assessment and evaluations of body temperature, and still has a significant impact on decisions in nursing care, medical diagnosis and treatment, and in the ordering of laboratory tests. Today, although there is a general acceptance that body temperature adopts a range of values rather than a fixed temperature, the norm arrived at in the mid-nineteenth century is still the basis for assessment and decisions about body temperature worldwide. In addition, even if the technical accuracy of measurements has become much better, *clinical accuracy*, meaning knowledge about physical influences on the individual's body temperature, such as thermoregulation and hormones, immunological defense against microbes, and the development of laboratory assays, is still not considered important for body temperature assessment. For example, due to the temperature gradients between different sites of measurement, it is impossible to measure or define the 'actual' body temperature as no factor exists which allows accurate conversion of temperatures recorded at one site to estimate the temperature at another. Also, in addition to the temperature differences between different sites in the same individual, there are considerable differences in body temperature between individuals, and therefore we have to assess changes in body temperature as the difference between an individual baseline body temperature and the measured reading, so-called DiffTemp™, and not use a predetermined, universal cut-off value.

When we say that someone has a 'fever', what do we really mean? In the first instance most people think of fever as equating to an elevated body temperature because of infectious disease. In fact, it is common to 'measure fever' more than to measure body temperature. However, fever is essentially defined as:

> a state of elevated core body temperature, which is often, but not necessarily, part of the defense of multicellular organisms (the host) against the invasion of live (microorganisms) or inanimate matter recognized as pathogenic or alien by the host. (IUPS TC. Glossary of Terms to Thermal Physiology. *Pflugers Archives* 1987, 410: 567–87)

Fever is thus part of a larger response in the body, in which many different cells are activated and react in what is called the acute phase response. This response does not mean that the body temperature is permanently elevated or that we experience the activity of the immune cells in the form of malaise. Immune cells may be continually active, day and night, without reaching the level of inflammation.

Taken together, a great deal is known about thermoregulation, and the factors influencing body temperature, from a technical and physiological viewpoint. It is of great importance to base the assessment and evaluation of temperature on evidence-based medicine and not on tradition or personal belief. Therefore, it is necessary to use knowledge from both of the two parallel lines and to integrate this knowledge to form a basis for evidence-based practice.

In order to use this knowledge in evidence-based practice, collaboration is necessary between professionals and between disciplines such as health care, laboratory science, and medical technology. In the clinical context, this means that health care personnel should work together to provide care which is both high quality and safe. This emphasizes the importance of teamwork and inter-professional learning (IPL), in the form of collaborative practice, inter-professional communication, and respect for one another's competence, so that the group may use their joint expertise to achieve excellence (Fig. 1.2).

The pedagogical approach of this textbook is problem-based learning (PBL). PBL is based on the acquisition of knowledge by problem-solving, using self-directed learning, and a scientific and critical approach. Here, the basis of PBL is inter-professional discussions of scenarios from clinical practice. Such discussion stimulates reflection, and the problem-solving process makes the knowledge accessible and easier to apply in real situations. Our intention with this textbook is that the reader will gain insight into the importance of using knowledge from different disciplines to develop an appreciation of the different aspects of body temperature. In addition, the reader will come to understand the concept of fever in a broader perspective than that traditionally adopted. The book is based on research in the fields of physiology, immunology, laboratory science, nursing care, metrology, technological and scientific developments, and measurement with clinical thermometers related to body temperature. In some chapters, well-established knowledge is presented, along with a recommendation for a general reference source such as a reputable textbook.

However, to understand today's ideas and concepts, we have to consider the perceptions of the past. Therefore, the book starts with two chapters (Chaps. 2 and 3) examining the historical perspective. The following chapters (Chaps. 4, 5, and 6) focus on technical measurement accuracy and on thermoregulation from a physiological and immunological

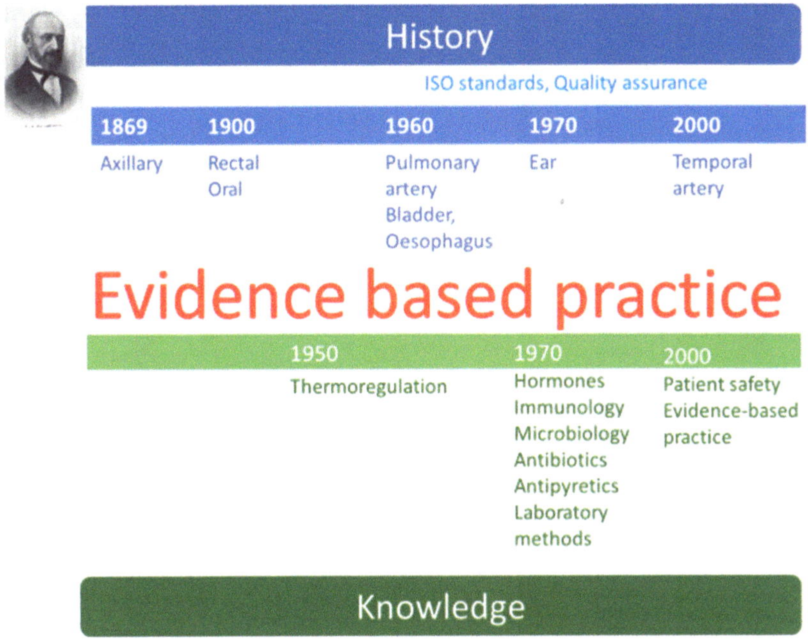

Fig. 1.2 Evidence-based practice based on integration of the two parallel lines of technique and physiological and immunological knowledge in relation to assessment of body temperature. (Copyright Grodzinsky, E & Sund Levander, M)

perspective. Chapter 7 addresses the assessment and evaluation of body temperature, and Chap. 8 looks at inflammatory activity in various conditions. In Chap. 9 we tie everything together and discuss how we can include evidence-based knowledge into clinical practice. In addition, all the chapters include thought clouds. It may not be possible to provide exact answers to the statements or questions in these clouds, but they are meant to encourage the reader's own reflections on the topic. At the end of each chapter there are also reflections, additional questions, and statements, which the reader should be able to answer using the text of the chapter. Throughout the book, we have converted °Celsius (°C) to °Fahrenheit (°F) according to the following formula:

$$^{\circ}\mathrm{C} \times 1.8 + 32 = ^{\circ}\mathrm{F}.$$

CHAPTER 2

History of Body Temperature

Ancient Times: An Imbalance in Bodily Fluids

In ancient times, diseases causing fever were thought to be due to an imbalance in the bodily fluids resulting from lifestyle or external factors such as the alignment of the stars or the climate. Fever was considered a healing, positive power but was also something dangerous for the body, and a punishment from the gods for evil conduct and an immoral lifestyle.

Hippocrates (460–357 BC) gave an explanation of the origin of disease based on the *humoral* theory, which interpreted the disease as an imbalance in the four body fluids: blood (red blood), black bile (coagulated blood), yellow bile (blood serum), and phlegm (fibrin). The body fluids were related to specific body organs and the four qualities of hot, dry, wet, and cold, and to the four elements in nature—fire, earth, water, and air—and these in turn were connected to the four seasons and also to human age. Thus, phlegm was related to the brain and old age, to water and winter; blood to the heart, infancy, air, and spring; yellow bile to the spleen, youth, fire, and summer; and black bile to the liver, maturity, earth, and autumn. When a person became ill, the relationship between the elements in the bodily fluids had been upset, and the natural balance was disturbed. By emptying out the harmful substance, the balance could be restored. Body and soul were linked together, as each body fluid was related to a specific temperament; phlegmatic (lethargic), sanguine (jovial), melancholic (melancholy), and choleric. A particular disease was explained as an increase in a bodily fluid and the individual temperament. For example,

E. Grodzinsky, M. Sund Levander (eds.), *Understanding Fever and Body Temperature*, https://doi.org/10.1007/978-3-030-21886-7_2

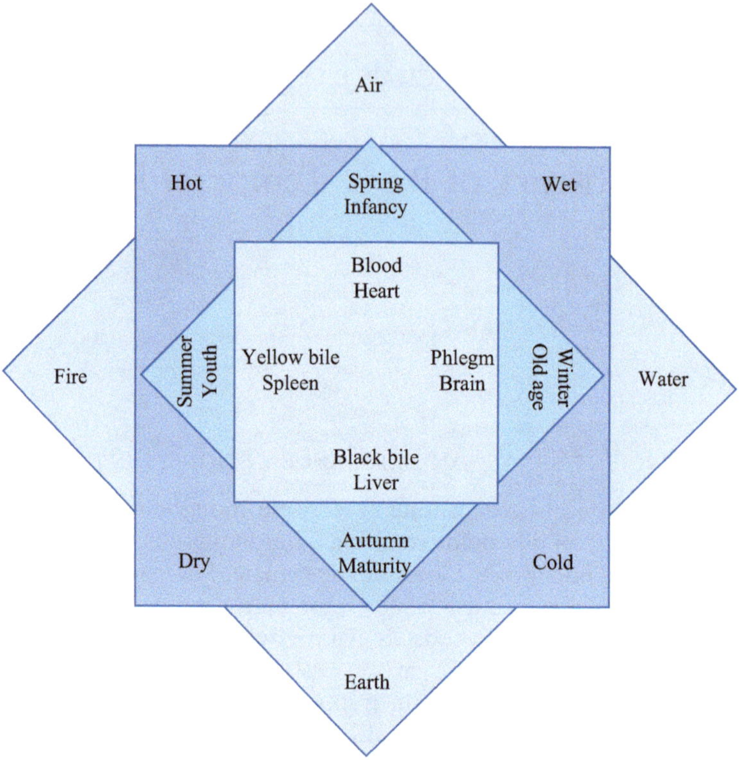

Fig. 2.1 The humoral theory. The relationship between the four qualities, elements, and humors, according to Hippocrates (460–357 BC). (Copyright Grodzinsky, E & Sund Levander, M)

fever was associated with an increase in yellow bile and the choleric temperament. A febrile disease was likened to fire—it was associated with both heat and drought. The physician's responsibility was to restore the balance and 'boil off' the excess or decrease blood volume by bloodletting or cupping (Fig. 2.1) [1, 2].

The humoral theory understood sweating as a means of excreting an excess or surplus from the body in order to restore balance. As fevered individuals began to recover, feel cooler, and indeed seem cooler to the observer's hand when they sweated, it was believed that the offending humors were leaving them in the sweat. Hence, according to the humoral theory, it was rational to encourage vigorous sweating during fever. The patient was wrapped up well and received infusions of herbs and roots to restore balance in the body fluids, for example, through sweating and vomiting. These principles for the treatment of fever have persisted [3] and are actually still used in practice, for example, opening windows to promote heat loss and 'sweating out' the fever.

Although the origins are not known, antipyretic therapy—cooling of the skin and pharmacological treatment—has been described since ancient times for treating fever. For example, the Babylonian physicians who tended Alexander the Great during the 8 days of febrile illness that ended his life in 323 BC prescribed repeated cool baths. Plants containing salicylic acid, such as the leaves and bark of willow trees, were recommended to treat inflammatory diseases and fever as early as 1500 BC, and later by Hippocrates. The ancient Chinese, and early Native Americans and Southern Africans, are also supposed to have used such treatment.

Long before the introduction of thermometers in clinical practice, ancient and medieval physicians recognized elevated body temperatures by dry, flushed, or hot skin. The first method for measuring body temperature has been attributed to Hippocrates.

> Soak a piece of fine linen in warm moist finely triturated Eretrian earth: then wrap this all the away round his thorax, and, wherever it first dries, that is where you must cauterize or incise, as close to the diaphragm as possible, but sparing the diaphragm itself. If you prefer apply the Eretrian earth directly and look for the place the same way you would in the linen; let many people apply the earth simultaneously, in order that the first applied does not become dry.

Hippocrates recommended this method to locate pulmonary infections; the hot area indicated inflammatory activity and hence was the place to make the incision [4].

Seventeenth Century: Accumulations of Waste Products and Fermentation

A breakpoint came at the beginning of the seventeenth century when the English physician William Harvey (1578–1657) proposed his theory of a closed circulatory system in the body. This posed a problem, as the humoral theory was based on the assumption of a slow movement of the blood, while Harvey suggested a rapid circulation. Harvey reconciled his theory with the old one and claimed that indigestion caused accumulations of waste products that hindered the blood from flowing freely. Fever was explained as the effect of boiling blood, when the body tried to reduce the waste. He claimed that nature itself healed most fevers. Nevertheless, he recommended a purgative in order to aid excretion of the waste. Another explanation related to this accumulation theory was that the heart had to beat faster and harder to overcome the blockage of the circulation, leading to an increased temperature and pulse. Later on, others explained this as a fermentation, either to dilute the foreign substances or to separate them from the blood [5].

Another theory claimed that fever was the effect of too much chemical fermentation in the blood, which caused the blood to boil off. It was also said that pulmonary waste products, which would normally disappear through the skin, were gathered in the blood, thereby causing fever. Yet another explanation was that blood was a depository for alkaline, acidic, and sulphurous bodies which normally counterbalanced each other. In illness, though, the balance was disturbed as one of them predominated. The balance was restored by giving the patient absorbents and emetics [5].

Thomas Sydenham (1624–1689) based his explanation on the humoral theory and claimed that fevers were caused by an imbalance in the four humors when the body was unable to break down certain particles that had undergone putrefaction, or which could not be assimilated into the bloodstream. Eruptions on the skin, diarrhea, and sweating were all methods for the body to eliminate those particles. To rectify the imbalance, the body was forced to increase disposal by incineration. This, in turn, brought about more heat and, ultimately, fever. Sydenham also believed in the force of Nature for healing illness, and that the seasons played a significant role in determining the nature of fevers. Hence, he recommended different treatments for different fevers and advocated bloodletting for spring fevers, but not for autumn fevers. In treating the plague, for example, Sydenham suggests,

> When the sick has been let blood, let him be covered all over with cloths and his forehead bound about with a piece of woollen cloth, and then if does not vomit, let some medicine to procure sweat be exhibited to him. [5]

In spite of some new suggestions, the general treatment of illness still aimed to restore the balance between the body fluids by excreting waste products. This was achieved by bloodletting, by promoting vomiting, or with enemas, cooling, or sweating. Commonly prescribed drugs were mercury, arsenic, and antimony [6].

Eighteenth Century: Thermoregulation and the Natural Phases of Fever

In the eighteenth century, the understanding of the causes and nature of fevers changed dramatically in response to scientific discoveries and medical observations such as thermoregulation. Even so, an increased temperature was still interpreted in terms of various febrile diseases, such as catarrhal fever, breast fever, stomach fever, decay fever, summer fever, autumn fever, burn fever, pain fever, fire fever, collapse fever, languishing fever, child languishing fever, bile fever, typhus fever, and rash fever [7]. Also, as with their ancient colleagues, eighteenth-century physicians still used touch as their main criteria to evaluate body heat [8]. The relation between fever and tachycardia was described by physicians as early as 300 BC, but it seems to have been forgotten until the eighteenth century, when it was again highlighted in relation to the speed of flow in blood vessels during fever [2, 8].

Also, the late eighteenth century saw the beginnings of an understanding of thermoregulation in terms of the body being cooled by perspiration. For example, James Currie (1756–1805) grasped the link between evaporation and cooling, and performed experiments of cooling and warming individuals, but could not explain what actually happened. He also asserted that human body temperature is between 36.1 °C (88.9 °F) and 36.7 °C (98.1 °F). Currie advocated measuring body temperature and also showed an intuition for choosing the correct time to start cooling the patient. He anticipated the natural course of fever and limited the use of cold-water treatment to occasions when the temperature was high but was likely soon to decline as the fever took its normal course. Hence, Currie understood the need to adjust any action to the natural phases of the fever. He also questioned the rationale for warming feverish patients and instead advocated cold drinks, cool air, and cooling of the skin. This regime for treating illness was in line with deep-rooted beliefs among lay people at that time, although cold baths for fever had been exceptional, if not entirely unknown. It is to Curries' credit that he clearly stated that cooling should never be used 'when any considerable sense of chilliness is present, even though the thermometer, applied to the trunk of the body, should indicate a degree of heat greater than usual'. The regime using cooling also spread to other continents, for example, when yellow fever raged in Philadelphia in 1793. However, the physicians in Philadelphia soon returned to the more traditional treatment, and some were pleased to state that 'not less than 6,000 of the inhabitants of Philadelphia probably owe their lives to purging and bleeding, during the autumn'. Traditional treatment still included opium for pain and drugs to restore imbalance in bodily fluids, such as ipecacuanha mixture for coughs and as an emetic, and antimony for sweating [3]. 'Wet cupping'—bleeding—along with venesection and leeches were other methods of treating illness. Bleeding was generally repeated once daily and continued until the patient fainted. An alternative was 'dry cupping' to produce blisters. Another treatment consisted of a purgative, rest, and a restricted diet [1]. In 1763, willow leaves were described as a successful treatment of malaria due to their antipyretic effect [9, 10].

An example of how fevers were treated at that time is the case of the 24-year-old servant George Kerr at the Royal Infirmary of Edinburgh. Kerr was admitted to the hospital in February 1789 for 'pyrexia, with headache, vertigo, nausea, anorexia, polydipsia, cough and pain in the chest'. To stimulate diaphoresis and diuresis he was first given a saline julep made with potassium carbonate, lemon juice, and blackcurrant syrup, and antimony to stimulate vomiting and catharsis. As no stool appeared, an enema was given the next day, and on three further occasions. This treatment was so effective that the physician had to prescribe opium to counteract the drug-induced catharsis. Kerr then became lethargic and therefore wine and Peruvian bark were added in order to strengthen his body tones. When he became delirious, the bark was discontinued as it was thought to be too strong for him. After about ten days, Kerr felt better and asked for porter and ale instead of wine. He was discharged after 23 days (Fig. 2.2) [8].

Although there were milestones along the way, such as understanding the closed system blood circulation and the relationship between pulse rate and temperature in the mid-seventeenth century, and the development of simple thermometers, it was not until the nineteenth century that thermometers began to be accepted. Physicians agreed that the pulse reflected body temperature, but they were not confident about thermometers, such as the one invented by Fahrenheit in 1714, and they were seldom used for measuring body temperature. Instead, they were used for estimating changes in outside temperature, as climate and the seasons were considered important for the incidence and understanding of fevers [5, 8]. An exception was the Scottish physician John Hunter (1728–1793), who argued

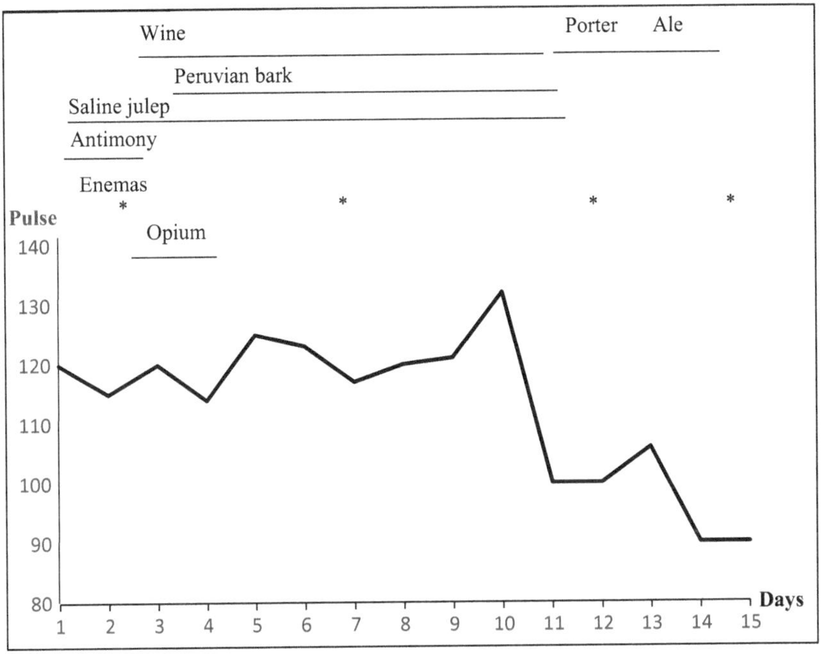

Fig. 2.2 Treatment of fever in February 1789: the case of George Kerr. (Modified from Estes, 1991 [8]. With permission from Grodzinsky, E & Sund Levander, M)

that thermometers should have a place in everyday practice [8]. Most physicians avoided thermometers, probably because axillary thermometers, which were the instrument of choice at the time, required at least 7 minutes, or even longer, to achieve equilibrium. The slow response was highly impractical, and some doctors noted the rate of rise rather than the final reading or added a supplement to the reading reached after a specified time, for example, 2° after 7.5 minutes [3]. This is probably the beginning of the tradition of adjusting measurement at different sites to one another.

Nineteenth Century: Medical Thermometers and 'Fever Hospitals'

A milestone in the assessment of body temperature was the introduction of medical thermometers into clinical practice during the mid-nineteenth century and the use of cards to record changes in the thermic curve over time. This was attributed to research done by the German physician Carl August Wunderlich (1815–1910), who measured the axillary temperature of thousands of patients and then defined a range for normal body temperature (see Chaps. 3 and 7) [11].

Even so, in the nineteenth century, the pulse rate still was the most important measure of fevers, which at this time were understood to be caused by spasm, or 'spasmodic affections', in the 'nervous' and vascular systems [8, 12]. For the physician, 'spasm' of the blood vessels was apparent by the patient's skin being pale and cold as the temperature rose, and by its redness and heat when the temperature fell [3]. Fever diseases were still regarded as by far the most dangerous and deadly diseases. Fever was divided into continued fever and periodic fever; the latter divided again into intermittent and remittent fevers, which were believed to be related to climate, season, and locality. As in the eighteenth century, the widely accepted concept of fever of the time still viewed fever as a general disease, which might assume various forms and become complicated by local inflammation in the body [13].

Fevers were associated with signs and symptoms such as pain in the lower back, cold and pale extremities, shivering, cardiac palpations, a small or weak pulse, dyspnea, violent headaches, restlessness, constipation, and a reduced output of urine and sweat [8]. The initial therapies were usually antiphlogistics, calming of the hyperactive cardiovascular or nervous systems, and avoiding activity and eating meat (which would 'feed' the fire of the inflammation). The patient was often given sedatives and diuretic and diaphoretic drugs in combination with bloodletting, cupping, and emetics in order to reduce the tension in the arteries. In order to stimulate the heart, cold water, Peruvian bark (quinine), alcohol, iron salts, and aromatic spices were used. In 1835, the French physician Luis observed that bloodletting in the early stages of pneumonia increased the mortality, especially in the elderly, and hence questioned the method [1]. Yet another recommendation was to place the patient in an upright position in the bath filled with warm water, and then pour cold water over him, for example, from a wooden bucket. Afterward the patient was scrubbed and dried and then put in a warm bed with a woolly nightcap to keep the shaven head warm [3]. The idea of the stomach as the principal source of innate body heat was suggested by Hunter in Edinburgh. He therefore argued that weakness of the stomach lowered temperature, supporting the admonition to 'feed a cold and starve a fever' [8].

In the later nineteenth century, the incidence of relapsing fever (malaria) was a major problem. Treatment was entirely limited to the reduction of excessive body heat with drugs, such as cinchona, quinine with camphor, or acetate of ammonia or by sponging with cold water. Arsenic, sulfites, hyposulfites, chlorine, or purgatives were not found to be effective against this disease [14]. Isolation of individuals with fevers and 'loathsome diseases' had been common since ancient times in order to protect society. In the latter part of the nineteenth century, isolation hospitals, also known as 'fever hospitals', were established to take care of diseased individuals. The nurses who took care of the patients were simply called 'fever nurses' [15]. In other areas, fever was used as a treatment: the curative effect of fevers on mental diseases had been described in ancient times, for example, to cure epilepsy and melancholy; and in the eighteenth century, fever was a treatment for 'madness'. In the nineteenth century, infectious diseases such as cholera, typhoid, acute exanthema, and erysipelas were observed to result in a temporary remission of hysterical attacks and psychosis. In the beginning of the twentieth century, malaria therapy was still being used for treating paralysis in the last stage of syphilis [16]. Also, toward the end of the nineteenth century, the possibility was raised that microbes might indirectly cause fever by releasing some sort of agent, probably secreted from the leucocytes, and having some kind of influence on the brain.

Interestingly, theories that fevers might be caused by poor living conditions were proposed by a handful of physicians early in the nineteenth century, as in this description from the Scottish physician William Alison in 1817:

> That the habits of the lower orders are in general very uncleanly, that many parts of the town, inhabited by them, are very close and dirty, that whole families, or even more that one, are often crowded into single rooms. Alison suggested cleanliness, fresh air, nourishing food, and isolation of fever patients at the Royal Infirmary of Edinburgh. [13]

This was in line with the suggestions made by Florence Nightingale (1820–1910) in the mid-nineteenth century, after her experiences in the Crimean War [17].

Twentieth Century: A Scientific Approach to Fever, Microorganisms, and Thermoregulation

At the beginning of the twentieth century, several scientists discovered that body temperature was regulated centrally in the hypothalamus. Now, a more scientific approach to the diagnosis and treatment of diseases, based on a more accurate knowledge of physiology, pathology, and microbiology, could be combined with old assumptions. Fever was explained as an elevated body temperature, caused by a combination of increased metabolism and inadequate heat loss. It was believed to cause accumulation of blood in the abdomen, explaining why the brain, skin, and muscles become anemic. It was further believed that the central nervous, respiratory, and circulatory systems, including the heart, could be paralyzed and that an extensive destruction of red blood cells could occur. It was also suggested that the cells of the body could be filled with grains, consisting in most cases of albumin but in others of fat [18].

Another explanation was that a rise in body temperature was due to three different causes. The first was mechanical interference with the normal function of the central nervous system, such as in neurological injuries; the second, interference with heat elimination, as is seen in heat stroke. The latter condition was explained by an accelerated rate of chemical change in the tissues, indicated by an increased excretion of carbonic acid. The third explanation was that products of microorganisms exert a toxic effect on animal protoplasm. It was also stressed that elevated temperature is not a disease in itself but rather is a symptom of disease [19].

In the early twentieth century, one rather different theory was suggested, namely that body temperature was not actually increased during fever but was lowered. This idea was based on the assumption that body heat was produced by the oxidation of food and by friction in the blood and lymph system. Some 'compensating action' balanced the relation between oxidation, friction, and the storage and excretion of body heat. A mathematical calculation based on the amount of material excreted from the body gave an estimation of increased or decreased body heat production. As there was no increase in the amount of excreta eliminated when febrile, there must be a state of decreased heat production, which needed treatment. Therefore, it was claimed that cold baths were contraindicated in fever [20].

However, by mid-century the regulation of body temperature was understood in terms of a balance between heat loss and heat production orchestrated by the hypothalamus. In the 1950s, though, the general opinion was still that high temperatures could damage tissues, which was questioned by DuBois, since people in good general condition could withstand 42 °C (107.6 °F) during fever therapy. He also reported the results of rectal temperature in 100 admitted medical patients and of 1761 readings in 367 patients, whose temperatures rarely exceeded 40.5 °C (104.9 °F) and never

41.2 °C (106.2 °F). Nevertheless, he stressed the importance of cooling the blood in the subcutaneous tissues as much as possible by cooling the room or the patient with sponges soaked in water or alcohol. Importantly, DuBois also pointed out that too great a chilling of the skin could lead to constriction of the peripheral blood vessels, reducing cooling of the internal organs, and raising the risk of shivering. He also described several conditions when body temperatures do exceed 41 °C (105.8 °F), such as sudden overwhelming heat load, as in fever therapy or reaction to pyrogens; exhaustion of the sweat glands, as in heat stroke; failure of the circulation or temperature regulation in moribund patients; and some infectious diseases which cause occasional high readings. His conclusion was that there must be some emergency mechanism that strongly resists temperature rises to levels which are life-threatening and that therefore the temperature in fever tends to remain safely below the danger point. Because DuBois also observed temperature gradients within the body, he stated that 'there is no one body temperature and it is impossible to determine accurately an average body temperature' [21].

At the beginning of the twentieth century, the widely accepted concept of fever still viewed it as a general disease, which might assume various forms and become complicated by local inflammation in the body [13]. Fever diseases were divided into continued fevers and periodic fevers, the latter further divided into intermittent and remittent fevers, which were believed to be related to climate, season, and locality and were still regarded as by far the most dangerous and deadly diseases. During the First World War, many soldiers became ill with fever while serving at the frontline. The fever was first explained from 'auto-intoxication' as a result of 'some change in the system' from the novel conditions of climate, living, and food. Later on, it was understood that this fever, named trench fever, resulted from hard work, combined with mud, rain, cold, and sleeplessness [22]. The treatment of trench fever combined purging with magnesium sulfate, followed by sodium salicylate and iron, arsenic, strychnine, and quinine three times a day, with rest in bed and a milk diet [22, 23].

Although fever was considered important to clear toxic substances from the bodily fluids, it was thought important to 'lead the fire right'. It was therefore advocated that 'as soon as the fever is found it should be treated' [18]. Skin activity was of paramount importance in the treatment of fever. The sickroom should have clean, cool air, preferably at 10 °C (50 °F) to 12 °C (53.6 °F), and the patient should receive a cool 'air bath' while avoiding freezing. In order to achieve an active extension of the skin vessels, water treatment was combined with rubbing of the skin, peeling, foot baths, and covering various parts of the body with wet packs, or turpentine, or flax seed poultices. Also, a mix of water and alcohol or vinegar was used to cool the body and sweat cures were employed, because perspiration was thought to secret toxins and increases urinary output, thus separating fever products and the fever toxin. This treatment would 'strengthen and enliven' both evaporation and thermal radiation from the body, which would stimulate the heart, skin activity, the nervous system, appetite, respiration, and excretion. Besides sweat cures, water enemas, bed rest, acidic beverages, and an easily digested diet were recommended—indigestible food could exacerbate the disease. Yet another piece of concrete advice was to 'go to bed and wrap you well, and when the bedclothes have been wet through, do a whole-body wash and then go to bed without wiping' [18, 23, 24]. This advice—that cooling of the body and concern for the stomach were significant in fever care—can also be found in manuals for housewives from the 1940s, with the addition that antipyretics are recommended [25]. At this time, antipyretic drugs were also incorporated to the clinical pharmacopeia [9, 10]. However, physicians did question the use of aspirin to reduce temperatures and diminish pain during fever [26].

Twenty-First Century: Interventions in Fever—Has Anything Changed?

The idea of using of bloodletting, cupping, leeches, and various more or less toxic substances to treat fevers is rare today. Interestingly, these techniques seem to have some real effects. Leeches secrete hirudin, a polypeptide with anticoagulant properties [1]. Another example is how bloodletting is related to the hormone vasopressin, which affects water balance and the cardiovascular system, as well as the increase in body temperature during fever. Both dehydration and hemorrhage are known to be potent stimulants of vasopressin from the brain into the circulation. Hence, the observations of Galen in AD 170 and Wunderlich in the twentieth century that a decrease in temperature resulted from bloodletting or natural bleeding such as from the nose or in menstruation could be due to vasopressin. In addition, the decline in bloodletting in the latter half of the twentieth century coincided closely with the use of the antipyretic drugs sodium salicylate and acetylsalicylic acid. Another effect of hemorrhage is a lowering of the iron levels in plasma, which decreases bacterial growth and replication and hence enhances healing [15].

Given the knowledge that now exists of the human immune system, the understanding of the causes of infectious diseases, and the development of medication for different infectious diseases, it would be natural to expect that interventions for increased temperature during fever had changed. However, descriptions from nurses illustrate that the tradition of cooling of the body and lowering body temperature during fever still persists: 'little bed linen, a cool room, wash with water or alcohol, sometimes combined with a fan, and antipyretics' [27].

Nurses' descriptions also show the lack of research-based nursing care for fever:

> You do what you have always done ... I think it's really up to me working and which patient I am responsible for.... We really have no procedures for what we are to do when the patient has a fever. [27]

The clinical implications of this will be addressed and discussed further in Chap. 9.

What about ancient ideas concerning fever today? Do these ideas still influence people today?

Hypothermia

That cold can have both injurious and beneficial effects on tissue has been known since ancient times. In addition to antipyresis against increased temperature in fever, the application of cold water and ice is still used to relieve pain and reduce swelling. Another field where hypothermia is induced is in cryosurgery, in which cold is applied locally for surgical procedures [28]. Warmth is also applied for pain relief, as well as in the treatment of skin tumors and infections. The beneficial effect of anti-infective thermotherapy is thought to involve direct toxic effects on microbes and/or upregulation of the body's immune response to the infectious agents [29].

The severe effects of hypothermia, including death, have been known for over 2000 years. Observations of extreme hypothermia in soldiers, such as when Hannibal crossed the Alps (218 BC) or during the Napoleonic wars (1799–1815), are documented in the literature. The word hypothermia originated in the late nineteenth century and was first described in relation to specific diseases, such as typhoid, cholera, pneumonia, and diphtheria, and to spinal cord injury. Hypothermia as a clinical syndrome could not be defined until the late nineteenth century when accurate temperature measurement became easier and normal temperatures had been defined. The treatment recommended at that time was to slowly rewarm the patient, who was laid on a mattress of horse-hair, then to massage the precordial region and the navel with ‘exciting tincture’, and after that to apply warm clothes. Later, the procedure was to use snow, iced water, and water slowly warmed, on the body. When respiration and circulation were sensibly restored, and the muscles felt tense, the patient should be wiped with dry linen, massaged with flannel, and then placed in bed, wrapped up in a woolen blanket. Later, stimulants such as tickling the nostrils with a feather, friction on the palm or sole with strong vinegar, and in severe cases electrical stimulation with a battery were used. As soon as they could swallow, the patient could be given spoonfuls of black or elderflower tea with some drops of ammonia, or a little brandy, or sweetened cinnamon wine [30].

Therapeutic hypothermia has probably been used for a long time, but clinical examples are documented only for the past 200 years. The so-called Russian method of resuscitation, described in 1805, meant that the patient was covered with snow in the hope of prompting a return of spontaneous circulation. Therapeutic hypothermia was also used during the Napoleonic wars in an effort to preserve injured limbs [31].

Reflections

- Reflect on how contemporary perceptions about fever have affected patient outcome and comfort.
- Reflect on how today’s perceptions of fever may affect patient comfort and outcomes.
- Reflect on the rationale for bleeding and cupping in modern medicine.

References

1. Turk JL, Allen E. Bleeding and cupping. His Med. 1981;65:128–31.
2. Atkins E. Fever- the old and the new. J Infect Dis. 1984;149(3):339–48.
3. Forrester JM. The origins and fate of James Currie’s cold water treatment of fever. Med Hist. 2000;44:57–74.
4. Otsuka K, Togawa T. Hippocratic thermography. Physiol Meas. 1997;18:227–32.

5. Sigal AL. Fever theory in the seventeenth century: building toward a comprehensive physiology. Yale J Biol Med. 1978;51:571–82.
6. Villner K. Blod, Kryddor och Sot (Blood, Spices and Sot) In Swedish. Stockholm: Carlssons Bokförlag; 1986.
7. Haartman J. Haartmans läkarbok av år 1765. Malmö: Örestads förlagstryckeri; 1963.
8. Estes JW. Quantitative observations of fever and its treatment before the advent of short clinical thermometers. Med Hist. 1991;35:189–216.
9. Mackowiak P. Brief history of antipyretic therapy. Clin Infect Dis. 2001;3.(Suppl. 5):54–6.
10. Mackowiak P, Plaisance K. Benefits and risks of antipyretic therapy. Ann N Y Acad Sci. 1998;29(856):214–23.
11. Mackowiak PA. History of clinical thermometry. In: Mackowiak PA, editor. Fever basic mechanisms and management. 2nd ed. Philadelphia/New York: Lippincott Raven; 1997. p. 1–10.
12. Atkins E. Fever: its history, cause, and function. Yale J Biol Med. 1982;55:283–9.
13. Wilson L. Fevers and science in the early nineteenth century medicine. J Hist Med Allied Sci. 1978;33(3):386–407.
14. Parry J. Observations on relapsing fever, as it occurred in Philadelphia in the winter of 1869 and 1870. Am J Med Sci. 1870;60:336–58.
15. Currie MR. The rise and demise of fever nurses. Int Hist Nurs J. 1997;3(1):5–19.
16. Whitrow M. Wagner-Jauregg and fever therapy. Med Hist. 1990;34:294–310.
17. Nightingale F. Anteckningar m Omvårdnad (Notes of nursing. What it is and what it is not). Stockholm: Emil Kihlströms Tryckeri AB; 1954.
18. Berg H. Läkarbok (Medical Book) In Swedish. Göteborg: Slanders Boktrycker; 1918.
19. Estill RJ. The significance of elevation of temperature. Ky Med J. July 1921:394–6.
20. Porter WH. Fever and what it really means. N Y Med J. 1919;CX(15):605–7.
21. DuBois EF. Why are fever temperatures over 106°C F rare? Am J Med Sci. 1948;217:361–8.
22. Costello JMA. Trench fever – mainly its clinical manifestation. In: Byam W, editor. Trench fever; a loose-born disease. London: Red Cross, U. S. American National red Cross/Medical Research Committee on Trench Fever; 1919. p. 456–66.
23. Hughes B. Trench pyrexia: their prevention and treatment. The Lancet. 1916;9:474.
24. Olvik O. Naturläkebok För Hemmet. Stockholm: Nutidens Förlags AB; 1925.

25. Anonymous. Husmoderns Lexikon (Housewife dictionary) In Swedish. Stockholm: Medens Förlag AB; 1966.
26. Robinson B. Practical points in the treatment of fever. Med Rec. 1919;17:818–9.
27. Sund Levander M, Wahren LK, Hamrin E. Nursing care in fever: assessment and implementation. Vård i Norden. 1998;18(2):27–30.
28. Gage AA. History of cryosurgery. Semin Surg Onchol. 1998;14:99–100.
29. Bayata S, Ermertcan T. Thermotherapy in dermatology. Cutan Ocul Toxicol. 2012;31(3):235–40.
30. Guly H. History of accidental hypothermia. Resuscitation. 2011;82:122–5.
31. Baron J. Therapeutic hypothermia: implications for acute care practitioners. Postgrad Med. 2010;122:19–27.

CHAPTER 3

History of the Thermometer

The temperature of the human body has been used as a diagnostic sign since the earliest days of clinical medicine. Hippocrates taught that the human hand can be used to judge the presence of fever as early as 400 BC, but instruments to measure this temperature were not developed until the sixteenth and seventeenth centuries. Even then, the journey to the routine measurement of temperature in clinical practice was a long one, with many different people contributing to the arrival of the small, inexpensive, and accurate instrument known throughout the world as 'the clinical thermometer'. A thermometer is essentially an instrument that can measure temperature. It detects changes in physical properties of an object or substance as the temperature of the object changes. The expansion and contraction of air with changes in temperature was noted as early as 220 BC by Philo of Byzantium. It was later realized that water also has this property, as do other fluids and metals such as mercury. As a result, there are now many different forms of thermometers which have been developed over a period of several hundred years.

Thermoscopy

The earliest thermal instruments were developed during the sixteenth and seventeenth centuries. These simple instruments were constructed so as to trap air in glass tubes with the open end of the tube submersed in a reservoir of water. These open thermometers were termed thermoscopes.

E. Grodzinsky, M. Sund Levander (eds.), *Understanding Fever and Body Temperature*, https://doi.org/10.1007/978-3-030-21886-7_3

In 1610, Galileo used wine instead of water and was one of the first to use an alcohol thermometer. It was, of course, found that when carrying such a device up a mountain to a different altitude that the level in the tube was affected by the changing atmospheric pressure. These devices illustrated changes in sensible heat, before the concept of temperature had been recognized. While it is sometimes claimed that Galileo was the inventor of the thermometer, what he actually produced was a thermoscope. He did discover that glass spheres filled with aqueous alcohol of different densities would rise and fall with changing temperature. Today, this is the principle of the Galilean thermometer, which is calibrated with a temperature scale.

The first illustration of a thermoscope showing a scale, which therefore can be described as a thermometer, was by Robert Fludd in 1638. However, around 1612, Santorio Santorio calibrated the tube and went on to attempt to measure human temperature with his thermoscope. At the end of the sealed tube, he had a bulb blown of the optimal size to be inserted in the mouth. The open end was submersed in fluid. As the air expanded due to the oral temperature, fluid was expelled from the tube. After a fixed period of time, the bulb was removed, the air cooled, causing the fluid to rise in the calibrated tube (Fig. 3.1) [1].

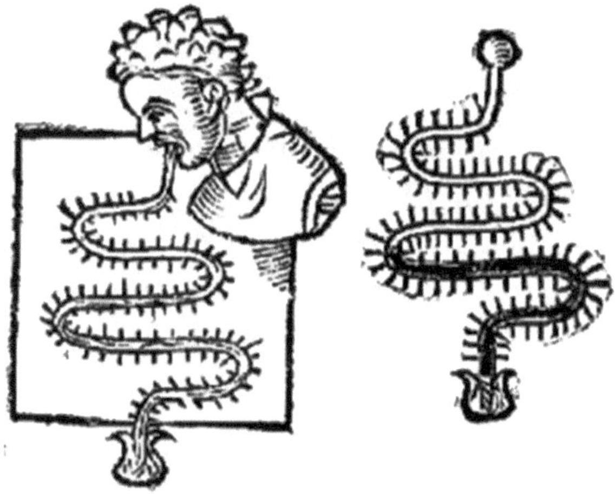

Fig. 3.1 A typical design of a thermoscope is a tube in which a liquid rises and falls as the temperature changes. The Sanctorius thermoscope. (With permission from Professor Francis Ring, the University of Leeds)

The Thermometer

In 1654, Ferdinand II de' Medici, Grand Duke of Tuscany, produced sealed tubes with a bulb and stem that were partly filled with alcohol. This was the first thermometer to depend on the expansion and contraction of a liquid, which was independent of barometric pressure. Many variants of this concept appeared, each unique as there was no standard scale. Christian Huygens in 1665 suggested using the melting point of ice and the boiling point of water as standards. The Danish astronomer Ole Rømer in Copenhagen used these upper and lower limits for a thermometer that he used to record the weather. There was still uncertainty about how well these parameters would work at different geographical latitudes. In 1694, Carlo Renaldini suggested that the ice and boiling water limits should be adopted as a universal scale. In England, Isaac Newton proposed in 1701 that a scale of 12 °C could be used between melting ice and body temperature!

The Fahrenheit Scale

In 1724, a German instrument-maker named Gabriel Fahrenheit produced a temperature scale that now bears his name. He manufactured high-quality thermometers with mercury (which has a high coefficient of expansion) with an inscribed scale with greater reproducibility. It was this that led to their general adoption. Fahrenheit first calibrated his thermometer with ice and sea salt as zero. Salt water has a much lower freezing point than ordinary water, so he chose the freezing point as 30 °F. The temperature inside the healthy human mouth was 96 °F, and he established the boiling point of water at 212 °F. He later adjusted his freezing point to 32 °F, so he established 180 °F between boiling and freezing which he measured at sea level [2].

The Centigrade Scale

In Uppsala, Sweden, Anders Celsius (1701–1741) had been involved in meteorological observations as an astronomy student. There were at that time a large number of different thermometers, all with different scales. He may have already at that early stage in his career realized that there was a need for a common international scale. He was appointed as professor of astronomy at Uppsala (as his father had been before him) and was involved in meteorological surveys. Celsius was the first to perform and publish careful experiments leading to the establishment of an international temperature scale based on scientific data. (He was for many years secretary of the Royal Society of Sciences at Uppsala.) His paper 'Observations of two persistent degrees on a thermometer' described his detailed experiments to check that the freezing point is independent of latitude and atmospheric pressure. He also determined the dependence of boiling water on atmospheric pressure and gave a rule for the determination of the boiling point if the barometric pressure deviates from a standard pressure [3].

Why would a student of astronomy be interested in scales of temperature measurement?

The position of zero was much discussed. The scale used by Ole Rømer placed zero at the lower temperature. Celsius had also used a thermometer created by the French astronomer Joseph-Nicolas Delisle with zero at the boiling point, thus giving a reversed scale with increasing numbers for decreasing temperatures, which avoided having negative values.

The reversal of this centigrade scale, placing zero at the freezing point, was inevitable and occurred a few years after Celsius's death. Various names are associated with this change. While Linnaeus is often credited, the history of thermometers in the proceedings of the Royal Swedish Academy of Sciences for 1749 mentions Celsius, his successor Strømer, and the instrument-maker Ekström in connection with the direct scale. No single person was given credit. A century later, Carl August Wunderlich stated in the English translation of his treatise on 'Temperature in Diseases' that he preferred to retain all his measurements in the centigrade scale, because the convenience of this scale will probably shortly lead to its general adoption by all scientific men. Celsius is now internationally recognized for his major contribution through his careful experiments and in using fixed points for calibration. This was recognized by the adoption in 1948 by an international conference on weights and measures of the preferred scale for temperature now referred to as degree Celsius (°C).

Imagine the setting for scientific discussions and the dissemination of new knowledge at the time of Linnaeus and Celsius.

The Kelvin Scale

In Scotland in 1848, Lord Kelvin realized in his study of heat that a much greater range of temperature could be considered, far beyond the centigrade scale. Absolute zero, the level at which all molecular motion stops, gives the lowest conceivable temperature that can be found. This he determined to be −273.16 degrees on the centigrade scale and −459.67 degrees on the Fahrenheit scale. Therefore, the lowest temperature on the Kelvin scale is 0, and the units are the same as the centigrade (Celsius) scale. While this scale is not used in clinical medicine, it may sometimes be used to define a temperature calibration source or similar scientific system.

Thermocouples

Thomas Seebeck, who was born in Estonia in 1770, is the person most closely associated with the thermocouple as a temperature-measuring device. In 1820, when at the Berlin Academy of Sciences, he had studied the magnetic influence of an electrical current. A year later, he announced his discovery that two different metals forming a closed circuit will display magnetic properties when there is a difference of temperature between the two points of contact. This, the Seebeck effect, is the basis of all thermoelectricity and led to the development of thermocouples for contact temperature measurement.

In recent years, this technology has been improved to provide highly accurate heat-measuring devices capable of measurement from a few degrees above absolute zero to high temperatures over 1600 °C (2912 °F). Their main applications generally fall outside the temperature range of the human body, but some patient-monitoring devices used in critical care employ thermocouples taped to the skin for continuous measurements over time. Thermocouples and thermistors are also used in sealed catheters for internal body temperature measurements [4].

Tympanic Membrane Radiometry

The first non-contact radiometer designed to measure body temperature in the inner ear canal was invented in 1964 by Theodor Benzinger. When doing research on human temperature regulation at the US Naval Medical Research Institute in Bethesda, Benzinger developed a small radiometer to measure as close as possible to the brain. This was intended to be a

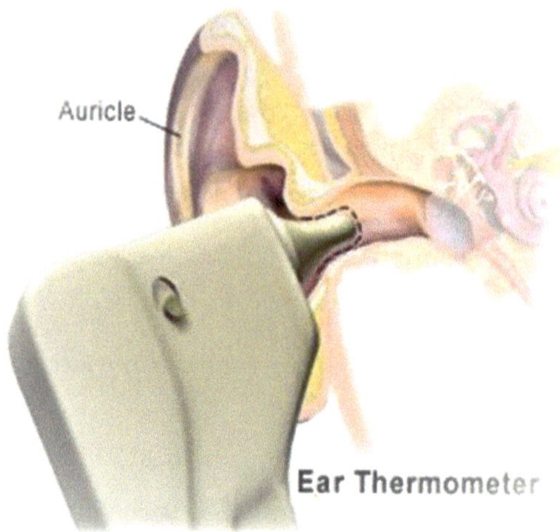

Fig. 3.2 Measurement of body temperature in the ear canal. (With permission from illustrator Jonny Hallberg, Sjöbo, Sweden)

non-invasive procedure, to avoid attaching electrodes to the hypothalamus [5]. The first systems were produced in the United States, Europe, and Japan in the early 1990s and have been increasingly adopted as a routine instrument for clinical thermometry (Fig. 3.2).

Clinical Thermometry

Since the earliest days of medicine, physicians have recognized that the human body can exhibit an abnormal rise in temperature, usually defined as fever, as an obvious symptom of certain illnesses. For example, the Bible has early references to fever in the Book of Job, and there are descriptions of 'burning bones' in the book of Psalms. Physicians were aware of the use of their hand as a standard means for estimating temperature. Hippocrates noted that the temperature of the body was important and insisted that physicians should be able to recognize the signs of abnormal temperature. He taught that steps should be taken to raise the temperature where it is depressed and lower it when raised. Galen (AD 131–201) described fever as *calor praeter naturam* or preternatural heat.

As already noted, the first attempts to measure the temperature of a human body seem to have occurred in the sixteenth and seventeenth centuries and then first in Italy. Giovanni Borelli, who had the support of Queen Christina of Sweden, was a pioneer of biomechanics and studied movement in animals. He is reputed to have tried many different measurements of the inner organs of live animals long before anaesthetics were available [6].

Santorio Santorio made an elaborate form of oral thermoscope to study human body temperature, although probably only with limited success.

Herman Boerhaave (1668–1738) and his pupils Gerard van Swieten and Anton de Haen noted the value of Fahrenheit's thermometer after it became available in 1714. Van Swieten became a professor of medicine at the University of Vienna and recommended that fever should be measured with a thermometer rather than with the hand. He applied the mercury thermometer to both the mouth and axilla as recommended by Fahrenheit. Anton de Haen taught clinical practice at the Vienna General Hospital and emphasized to all his students of the importance of measuring body temperature in fever. He pointed out that a physician's touch was inadequate, especially when a shivering patient complained of extreme coolness while registering a temperature that was three or more degrees above normal. Unfortunately, his studies were scattered throughout his 15 volumes of publications, *Ratio Medendi* (1757–1773). These included observations on temperature related to diurnal fluctuations, in the elderly, and on the action of certain drugs. De Haen's detailed observations, just part of his extensive work, went largely unheeded [7].

Excellent work on the temperature of healthy people and animals had been published by George Martine (1702–1741), a physician who had studied in Edinburgh and Leiden. He theorized that animal heat was the result of the velocity of blood moving through the vessels. His work inspired many others including John Lining in 1748 on temperature in those suffering from malaria, and John Hunter (1728–1793) one of the great surgeons and pioneers of the circulatory system. Hunter subsequently disagreed with Martine, claiming that 'warmth depends on a different principle, which is intimately connected with life itself, and is a power which maintains and regulates the machine, independent alike of the circulation, the will, and of sensation' [2].

Many of the early thermometers were of doubtful accuracy, and frequently they were inconveniently large. However, by 1835 Becquerel and Breschet were able to establish the mean temperature of a healthy adult to be 37 °C (98.6 °F). By the 1860s, the use of the thermometer had become more common, and the physiological significance of body temperature was becoming clearer. By 1863, John Davy had noted the variations in temperature resulting from exercise, the intake of food and drink, the influence of external temperature, and the differences in body processes in children. By this time, it was recognized that in many situations, temperature was a better clinical indicator than the pulse, because it was not affected by nervous activity or excitement.

Reflect on the statement that body temperature is not affected by nervous activity or excitement.

During this period of increasing interest in thermometry, Carl Reinhold Wunderlich (1815–1910) published his major work on *Temperature in Diseases* when at Leipzig in 1868. This was published in an English translation in 1871 [8]. His treatise was based on regular temperature measurements made on all his patients over the course of 15 years, some as many as four to six times daily. After some 100,000 observations, Wunderlich showed that when the temperatures were plotted on charts, the disease could be shown to follow certain laws, which could be characterized by the trend in temperature. Overall, he studied some 25,000 specific cases. This was clearly a significant contribution to the subject and places Wunderlich at the forefront of discovery in this aspect of clinical observation. He had established that the temperature in a healthy person is constant and that variation of temperature occurs in disease. From this, Wunderlich laid down a code based on principles that he had derived from his large set of observations. By this time it was considered that 'a physician who carried on his profession without the thermometer was like a blind man endeavouring to distinguish colours by feeling'.

In the first chapter of his book, Wunderlich lists 40 precepts of human body temperature, most of which remain unchallenged in modern medicine. Here are some examples:

The temperature of healthy person is almost constantly the same, although not absolutely. So, indeed there are spontaneous variations in the course of every twenty-four hours, but these seldom exceed half a degree of the centigrade scale.

A normal temperature does not necessarily indicate health, but all those whose temperature either exceeds or falls short of the normal range are unhealthy.

The range of temperature in the most severe diseases is between 35 °C (95 °F) and 42.5 °C (108.5 °F), and it is very seldom that it exceeds 43 °C (109.4 °F) or sinks below 33 °C (91.4 °F).

Alterations of temperature may be confined to special regions of the body, which are the seat of disease actions (local inflammation), while the general temperature remains more or less normal.

A rapid increase in temperature of the body from a chill, or in the normal warmth of the hands, feet, nose, or forehead, is commonly associated with strong feelings of chilliness and convulsive movements ('cold shivers', rigors, 'fever-frost').

A more or less permanent and noticeable rise in temperature amounting to 38.5 °C (101.3 °F) or more, is generally accompanied with subjective feelings of heat, and lassitude, as well as with thirst and headache...and rapidity of the pulse ...('feverishness', pyrexia, fever).

When there are extremes of temperature, we know that there is great danger. High fever is indicated by temperatures above 39.5 °C (103.1 °F) in the morning, and above 40.5 °C (104.9 °F) in the evening.

Temperatures in every known disease except relapsing fever, in all probability, indicate a fatal termination (42 °C [107.6 °F] or more-hyperpyretic temperatures).

Abnormally low temperatures may seriously disturb the various functions of the body; and when the fall is very considerable, it may render the continuation of life impossible [8].

These extracts are abridged from the very detailed description of differing types of fevers that were accepted in nineteenth-century medicine. In the full text of *Temperature in Diseases*, Wunderlich provides a most comprehensive list of investigators, mainly German and European, who had studied the role of thermometry in man and animals. He also discusses the various sites on the human body where thermometry may be applied. Of the many potential areas, he showed that in the hand or between fingers and toes was too unreliable. Rectal and vaginal sites were also criticized, the former being affected by masses of faeces, and the latter lacking in clinical evidence of reliability. The axilla and the mouth were advocated, with warnings of the effects of ingestion of food and drink, and or oral breathing when suffering from nasal congestion.

Much of this work by Wunderlich and others was performed with large, slow thermometers sometimes requiring 20 minutes to fully register. The need for a narrow temperature range of clinical thermometer was obvious. This should also be a maximum registering thermometer, small in size, and able to be fitted into a protective case. In this way a physician could carry a stethoscope and a thermometer in his personal kit, thus increasing the use of temperature measurement in diagnosis.

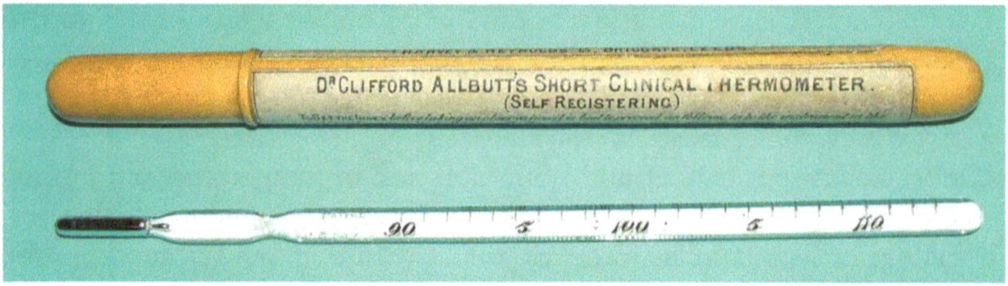

Fig. 3.3 Allbutt's clinical mercury thermometer. (The Museum of the History of Science, Technology and Medicine at the University of Leeds. Photo and with permission from Professor Francis Ring, the University of Leeds)

The Clinical Thermometer

While different names have been associated with the arrival of the 'clinical thermometer', the Allbutt clinical thermometer was the first practical device to become commercially available. Sir Thomas Clifford Allbutt (1836–1925) was a celebrated British physician. He spent 20 years working in Leeds during which time he devised the small clinical thermometer. A local company, Harvey and Reynolds, first manufactured this special thermometer in 1867, followed by Thackeray in London. Allbutt made the design of his thermometer freely available to others, and it was quickly taken up by British physicians. It was notable in that the instrument, 15 centimetres long, had a constriction in the capillary tube that held the mercury at its reading after use, until shaken down to the lower limit of calibration (Fig. 3.3).

The temperature reading was available in 5 minutes and initially was calibrated to 90–110 degrees on the Fahrenheit scale (32–43.3 °C). Later clinical thermometers were marked with the centigrade scale. Thomas Allbutt made several significant contributions to medicine, including the ophthalmoscope. He received royal recognition in England, being awarded a knighthood in 1907, and he was made the president of the British Medical Association in 1920 [9, 10].

Non-contact Temperature Measurement

Although William Herschel in Britain had identified the existence of infrared radiation in 1800, it took many years for remote heat sensing to be developed. Throughout the 1930s and 1940s, this technology came into practical use, accelerated by the needs of the military during the Second World War. In the late 1950s, once infrared technology had been declassified, thermal imaging became available to medicine and industry. Although the early systems were slow scanners, it became clear that it was possible to record the temperature distribution of a human subject or an object. An important conference in 1964 at the New York Academy of Sciences revealed the true potential of this technology in the study of human body temperature [11].

Also, in 1964 the German physician Dr Theodore Benzinger, who had moved to the United States, developed a small radiometric device to measure the temperature of the inner ear (tympanic membrane). In contrast to the very expensive early thermal imaging systems, this device promised a low cost and reliable means of measuring temperature close to the brain, but without the invasive contact of thermocouples. Initially only used for military and space technology, the tympanic radiometer came into medicine some 30 years later. This was undoubtedly stimulated by the concerns about the use of mercury on thermometers and its subsequent banning. The radiometer was further developed in the United States for measuring temperature over the temporal artery and was also used to measure forehead temperature. The latter application is not always successful, as the forehead may be a site of profuse sweating, either from physical exertion or from fever.

Why temperature measurements in space?

After 50 years of ever-improving and cheaper thermal imaging, its use is still growing in medicine [12]. A significant chain of events during the severe acute respiratory syndrome (SARS) outbreak and subsequent pandemic threats of the Hemagglutinin and Newaminidase (HN) viruses has resulted in trials using thermal imaging of the face for airport screening of the travelling public. This has led to the International Standards Organization publishing documents to highlight the essential requirements of thermal imaging cameras and their optimal use in this application. From this work, it is now established that a close-up thermogram of the subject's frontal face can be used to measure the temperature of the inner canthus of the eye and so to detect fever by remote sensing (see Chap. 3) [13, 14].

Thus, the study of human body temperature continues to evolve, and the technology applied to it is still being developed [15]. Many pioneers in medicine, physiology, and the physical sciences have contributed to this story, which, inevitably, cannot be said to be over. Our knowledge of the science of the human body will doubtless continue to grow, yet the long centuries of battles against human disease have not yet come to an end.

Reflections

- Reflect on Wunderlich's statements about body temperature from 1869. Are these statements still valid?
- Reflect on the influence Wunderlich might have on current opinions on body temperature.
- Reflect on the accuracy of devices from the past, in terms of reliability, repeatability, and operator performance.
- Reflect on why changes in body temperature have become so important in assessing health and disease.
- Reflect on whether the focus on measuring body temperature exactly might have affected clinical practice.

References

1. Santorio S. Ars de Statica Medicina. Leipzig: Schurer, Z & Gotz, M; 1614.
2. Haller JS. Medical thermometry – a short history. West J Med. 1985;142:108–16.
3. Collinder P. Swedish astronomers 1477–1900 Acta Universitatis Upsaliensis. 1970;Ser. C.
4. Hunt L. The early history of the thermocouple. Platin Met Rev. 1964;8:23–8.
5. Benzinger M. Tympanic thermometry in anaesthesia and surgery. J Am Med Assoc. 1969;209:1207–11.
6. Duck F. Physicists and physicians. York: Institute of Physics and Engineering in Medicine; 2013.
7. de Haen A. Ratio Mendendi in Nosaocomio Practico Vindobonensi. Vienna: Kruckten; 1757–1773.
8. Wunderlich CA, Seguin E. Medical thermometry and human temperature. New York: William Wood & Co; 1871. 280 p
9. Albutt T. Medical thermometry. Br Foreign Med Chir Rev. 1870;45(90):429–41.
10. Albutt T. Medical thermometry. Br Foreign Med Chir Rev. 1870;46(91):144–56.
11. Whipple H, editor. Thermography and its clinical applications. New York: New York Academy of sciences; 1964.
12. Ring E, Ammer K. Infrared thermal imaging in medicine. Topical review. Physiol Meas. 2012;33:R33–46.
13. ISO. Medical electrical equipment_Part 2-56: particular requirements for basic safety and essential performance of clinical thermometers for body temperature

measurement. Switzerland: ISO/TC 121/SC 3 Lung ventilators and related equipment; 2017.
14. ISO. Medical electrical equipment: deployment, implementation and operational guidelines for identifying febrile humans using a screening thermography. Geneva: International Electro-technical Commission; 2009.
15. Ring E, Hartmann J, Ammer K, Thomas R, Land D, Hand J, editors. Radiometric temperature measurement. Amsterdam: Elsevier/Academic Press; 2010.

CHAPTER 4

Technical Accuracy

Calibration

Temperature is a measure of the hotness or coldness of an object, where hot has a higher 'temperature' than cold. Several units of temperature have been suggested over the centuries, and today the most common are the Celsius, Fahrenheit, and Kelvin scales. The two formers are common units of temperature used by the public, and the latter is the SI unit of thermodynamic temperature (SI from the Système International d'unités, or international system of units). One Kelvin is defined as the fraction 1/273.16 of the thermodynamic temperature of the triple point of water—the unique temperature at which the three phases of water are in equilibrium. This fixed point is the basis for the International Temperature Scale (ITS) [1]. The measurement of temperature is a well-established field of metrology (measurement science), which broadly divides into two practical methods of implementation: contact and non-contact thermometry [2]. Non-contact thermometry, unlike contact thermometry, is a modern technique that has developed significantly over the last 50 years (see Chap. 3). Improved understanding of the theoretical aspects of the technique, along with improved technology, has increased its practical application. Of particular impact in the healthcare sector has been the now widespread use in clinical centres of non-contact thermometry—infrared (IR) radiation thermometry—for body temperature measurement [3], for example, using IR ear thermometers (IRETs).

E. Grodzinsky, M. Sund Levander (eds.), *Understanding Fever and Body Temperature*, https://doi.org/10.1007/978-3-030-21886-7_4

Calibration is the process of attributing a traceable temperature to the output of a thermometer. For example, an IR radiometer has a detector sensitive to IR radiation and is only an IR radiation thermometer when it has a traceable temperature attributed to its output. In order to confirm that instruments used for temperature measurement are performing reliably for their given application, it is critical that they are regularly calibrated [4, 5]. The calibration of a thermometer is typically performed 'by comparison' against a standard source of known temperature. A standard source provides a known reference against which the instrument output can be validated. In order to determine the full performance of an instrument, a number of calibration reference sources are used in order to cover the working range of the instrument under calibration (Fig. 4.1) [6, 7].

Measurement in itself is objective, in that a device only measures its own temperature and nothing else. However, the question may always be asked, what is it that it is being measured against? In other words, what is the measurement reference or standard? In the case of temperature measurement, a number of scales have been adopted over the centuries, most notably those first proposed by Fahrenheit and Celsius. These scales were developed in

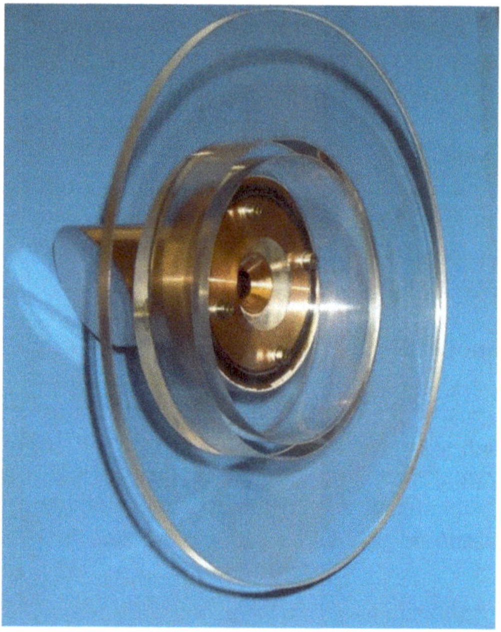

Fig. 4.1 The CENELEC European Standard (CEN) blackbody radiator (copper) mounted in a plastic fitting to enable immersion in a stirred liquid bath. (With permission. © NPL Management Ltd., 2019, London, UK)

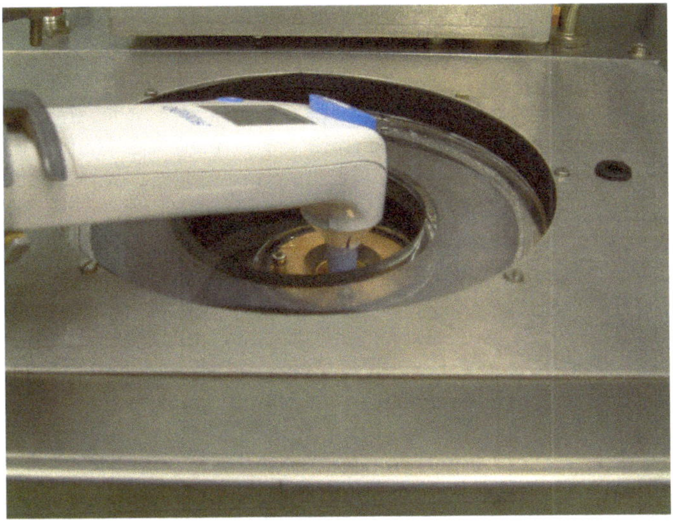

Fig. 4.2 A tympanic (ear) thermometer undergoing calibration against a high-precision blackbody reference source in accordance with the CENELEC European Standard (CEN) guidelines. (With permission. © NPL Management Ltd., London, UK)

tandem with particular thermodynamic fixed points (such as the melting point or boiling point of water). The usefulness of a phase change of a pure substance has led to the specification of several melting and freezing points of various pure substances, and these now help to define the International Temperature Scale of 1990 (ITS-90) [1] (Fig. 4.2) [6, 7].

Traceability, Accreditation, ITS-90, and Standards

The traceability of a thermometer to an internationally recognised temperature is ensured when a measurement can be demonstrably related to a common standard. For temperature, this means that there is an unbroken chain of measurements running back to the International Temperature Scale of 1990 (ITS-90) and that this can be demonstrated. The traceability of the calibration reference source is critical. The traceability of a source is passed by means of calibration to the instrument. It is important that every measurement instrument is traceable to ITS-90. Without this essential step, a number of independent temperature scales would be established, derived from the different sources against which the instruments were calibrated. Then when international, national, or regional comparisons are made, the results will not be compatible.

Accreditation is an independent, objective means of reviewing calibration facilities, procedures, and staff. A third party (e.g., the United Kingdom Accreditation Service in the case of the United Kingdom) reviews and assesses the staff, records, standards, and procedures used to carry out calibrations. The third-party assessment ensures that the calibration provider is producing a traceable, and therefore internationally accepted, calibration service. Accreditation meeting the International Organisation for Standardisation standard ISO-17025 (ISO/IECI 1999) [8], in terms of temperature calibration, means that the calibration provided to the user is demonstrably traceable to ITS-90 by an unbroken chain of measurements.

Thus, ITS-90 is the international measurement community's accepted approximation to thermodynamic temperature. It constitutes an internationally agreed scale, set up using several defined temperature fixed points and thermometers for interpolation. The text of ITS-90, governing the fixed points, their attributed temperature values, the forms of the measurement instruments, and interpolation equations, provides all the essentials for the establishment of an internationally agreed scale. The specification standard that governs clinical thermometers in Europe is EN 12470-5 [9], while its international equivalents are ASTM E-1965 [10] and JIS T 4207 [11]. Each part of EN 12470 defines the main terms it uses and the type of thermometer in question. Part 1 is concerned with metallic liquid-in-glass thermometers with maximum device, Part 2 covers phase change-type (dot matrix) thermometers, Part 3 is about the performance of compact electrical thermometers (non-predictive and predictive with maximum device), Part 4 focuses on the performance of electrical thermometers for continuous measurement, and Part 5 considers the performance of infrared ear thermometers with maximum device. The standard sets out to ensure that all clinical thermometers in use in Europe are fit for purpose with respect to temperature range, resolution, accuracy (maximum permissible error), response time, stability, environmental operating conditions, construction, and electrical and mechanical safety. The standard also specifies the procedures and apparatus which the manufacturer must use to test thermometer performance, either by individual testing or by testing a sample of thermometers selected according to a specified procedure. Finally, it specifies how the results must be expressed and what information has to be provided to the customer. In the case of a compact electrical thermometer, for example, it must:

cover a minimum measuring range from 35.5 °C (95.9 °F) to 42.0 °C (107.6 °F) with a maximum permissible error of 0.1 °C (32.2 °F) in an ambient temperature between 18 °C (64.4 °F) and 28 °C (82.4 °F),

reach the final temperature in no more than 60 seconds,

remain within the specification after exposure to a temperature of 55 °C (131 °F) for 12 days or 80 °C (176 °F) for 4 days,

have a digital display increment of 0.1 °C (32.2 °F) or less with digits at least 4 mm high, and

be calibrated in specified conditions using a standard thermometer with an uncertainty not greater than ±0.02 °C (32 °F).

Consider the pros and cons of the system of standards. Imagine using a device that does not conform to any standard.

Clinical Thermometers

Clinical thermometers can be of two main types: direct mode or adjusted mode (see Chap. 7). In the direct mode, the temperature displayed by the thermometer corresponds to the true temperature of the measurement site where the thermometer is placed. The thermometer sensor and the measuring site come into thermal equilibrium or have nearly the same temperature. The accuracy of a direct-mode clinical thermometer can be verified in the laboratory using a reference temperature source [4–7].

In an adjusted-mode thermometer, the thermometer's temperature reading is not necessarily the same as the temperature measured by the sensor. The output is the result of a signal adjustment or conversion, where the adjustment reflects the anatomical and physiological properties of the human subject as well as environmental conditions. Consider the following:

An IR ear thermometer which measures the thermal radiation from the ear canal but displays the patient's rectal temperature. Because of the conversion, the result displayed is strictly speaking only an estimate of the rectal temperature.

An IR ear thermometer which measures the thermal radiation from the ear canal but displays the patient's oral temperature. In this case, the oral temperature is estimated by adjusting the results of the measurement of the ear canal temperature.

A predictive clinical thermometer. This type takes several data points over time and uses the rate of change of the temperature along with a mathematical algorithm to calculate the expected final temperature. By anticipating the final temperature, the measurement time can be shortened from minutes to seconds. The thermometer maintains the calculated maximum temperature value for a specified time or until reset by the user.

It should be noted that some thermometers have a 'maximum device' that stores and maintains the maximum temperature reading until it is reset by the user. For example, a metallic liquid-in-glass thermometer with maximum device prevents the liquid column from falling when the thermometer is removed from the mouth, enabling the thermometer to be read more easily. Clinical electrical thermometers also display the maximum reading until reset.

General Principles of Operation

All clinical thermometers have at least two essential components: a sensor and some means of displaying the output of the sensor—for example, a digital display. The sensor is incorporated into the probe, and the probe is placed so that it is thermally coupled to the measurement (body) site. The sensor converts thermal energy from the measurement site into an electrical signal from which the temperature of the measurement site can be determined. Thermometers can either be so-called contact devices, where the thermometer is in direct contact with the body site, or 'non-contact devices' or infrared, where the temperature is estimated by infrared radiation [2, 12, 13]. An example of a contact thermometer is an electrical pencil thermometer for sublingual measurements; an example of a non-contact thermometer is the tympanic (or ear) thermometer. Contact thermometers come into thermal equilibrium with the body site, while non-contact thermometers measure the infrared radiation emitted by the surface of the body site.

Clinical thermometers are required to provide an accurate indication of patient temperature to ensure correct diagnosis and treatment. They have to be fit for purpose and suitable for the use for which they are intended, meaning, for example, that they must be small enough to be correctly inserted into the measurement site, and they must be safe to use and not cause injury to the patient. Different types and designs of thermometer exist for different applications and for different patient groups. There are a number of issues with accuracy, stability, and repeatability and the like associated with their use in a clinical environment, and users need to be aware of them [5].

Accuracy refers to the assessment of whether a thermometer can provide an accurate reading in use and can only be assessed by comparing the thermometer to a known reference source, for example, a calibration source traceable to ITS-90 [1]. The question of accuracy in clinical practice is discussed below.

Stability is related to the clinical context, because a patient's body temperature is measured in part to analyse and monitor their condition. It is therefore critical that a thermometer should, above all, be accurate. In addition, if it is to be used for patient monitoring, it must also be stable in both the short and long term. If the thermometer is not stable, monitoring the patient is useless, if only because an observed drift in patient temperature may well be caused by the thermometer. Alignment, ambient temperature variations, or procedural measurement issues can all cause discrepancies when taking regular readings. The most suitable form of stability analysis is a comparison of the thermometer against a standard reference source traceable to ITS-90 [1].

Repeatability is the ability of a measurement device, when measuring a known source, to return the same measurement value in repeated measurement cycles. The repeatability of a thermometer is critical if it is to be used as a medical diagnostic device. The thermometer must be able to produce, under the same conditions, repeated readings that differ only by the uncertainty given for that thermometer. The most suitable form of repeatability analysis is a comparison of the thermometer against a standard reference source traceable to ITS-90 [1].

These instrument measurement performance characteristics—accuracy, stability, and repeatability—are the ones typically assessed in the periodic calibration of the instrument [5, 12].

Other Factors Affecting Measurement

Beyond the fundamental temperature measurement performance and assessment of the thermometer obtained through regular calibration, there are a number of performance-related factors that should be noted for the thermometer 'in use'. For example, there are possible issues with thermometer time response—in other words, the length of time it takes for the thermometer to come into thermal equilibrium with the measurement site before a reading can be taken. Care should be taken to begin measurements only once the reading is stable. A predictive oral thermometer, for example, takes several data points over a defined period of time and uses the rate of change of the temperature along with a mathematical algorithm to calculate the expected final temperature. The measurement time is shortened from minutes to seconds since the equilibrium temperature is anticipated. However, some studies have suggested that the improvements in safety, speed, and ease of use provided by newer digital thermometers have been offset by a loss of accuracy and reliability compared to traditional mercury-in-glass thermometers. Furthermore, as calibration baths do not respond in the same way as human physiology, there are implications when calibrating the devices.

Imagine a device that requires at least three minutes to achieve equilibrium, but in all other matters is perfect.

Probe covers have been introduced to reduce cross-contamination, and their use adds further complications to the measurement. Since tympanic thermometers sense thermal radiation through the probe cover, correct use of the probe cover is particularly important. If the probe cover is damaged, this could affect the thermometer reading. If the cover is not attached correctly, differences in reading can occur, possibly as a result of air gaps between the cover and the probe. This will result in a lower reading, and more variation between readings. If an incorrect probe cover is used (one with different optical properties), again an incorrect reading may result.

Some thermometers are sensitive to being warmed up while being held in the hand (hand heating) due to the location of the sensing element and the poor thermal isolation of the sensor. This results in a thermometer reading that gradually changes as the instrument warms up. In addition, a similar effect can be observed when an instrument is taken from one thermal environment (i.e., outdoors) to another thermal environment (indoors). These changes in environmental temperature and/or heating by the user's hand can lead to erroneous results. Hence, it is of great importance to read the user manual, which often states (a) the environmental conditions for use and (b) the procedures to follow when the thermometer is taken from one thermal environment to another. These should always be adhered to.

Sufficient time should be allowed between placing the thermometer at the measurement site and reading the thermometer in order to allow the thermometer to reach thermal equilibrium. If insufficient time is allowed, the thermometer may not display the correct temperature. The required insertion time depends on the thermometer. Again, the manufacturer's instruction manual will often give the procedures for insertion. These should always be adhered to.

It is critical for successful measurement that the thermometer is correctly placed at the measurement site. If not, the reading may well be erroneous. For example:

For tympanic (ear) thermometers, the thermometer should be inserted into the ear canal so that it views the tympanic membrane correctly.
For oral thermometers, the thermometer must be inserted into one of the sublingual pockets.
For axillary measurements, the thermometer should be placed centrally within the patient's axilla (armpit).
For forehead (temporal artery) thermometers, the thermometer should be placed flat on the centre of the forehead and moved across the forehead, in contact with the skin, until it reaches the hairline.
For rectal thermometers, the thermometer should be inserted 5 cm in adults and 3 cm in children.

The manufacturer's instruction manual will often give recommended procedures for the correct placement of the instrument. These should always be adhered to. Before using a clinical thermometer, it is necessary to make sure that it is reading accurately—in other words that it is correctly calibrated. Between calibrations, the thermometer must be maintained in such a way as to keep it fit for its designed purpose—to measure patient temperature. It must not be dropped or mishandled, and if it is, checks must be carried out before it is used to make sure that it is still operating correctly. Before using a thermometer, a visual check is recommended to make sure that there is no obvious sign of damage.

Types of Thermometers

There are many different types of clinical thermometers available [13], of which the most common systems in clinical use for body temperature measurement are detailed here. There are also some very specific thermometers used in medicine (such as oesophageal, catheter, and pulmonary artery thermometers) but these devices are not covered here. (For more about temperature measurement and thermometers, see Chap. 7.)

Clinical mercury and liquid-in-glass thermometers are the familiar devices with a small glass bulb containing a reservoir of mercury or other suitable liquid attached to a stem with a narrow bore. The length of the mercury thread in the bore varies with the temperature because of thermal expansion and contraction, and the temperature can be read from a scale marked on the stem. The thermometer is placed at the measurement site and allowed to reach thermal equilibrium. The time the thermometer requires to come into thermal equilibrium can be a number of minutes.

Most clinical electrical thermometers are configured to display the maximum temperature, but some are 'continuous-reading', following the temperature changes up and down. Being electrical, these thermometers can be simply interfaced with instrumentation to display and record the temperature over longer periods. Electronic probe thermometers are generally faster than mercury-in-glass thermometers and save nursing time. However, it has been suggested that their faster response leads to a loss of accuracy and reliability. The reduced time for measurement is predominantly due to the implementation of predictive measurement, in which several data points are captured over a defined time period, and the rate of change of the temperature, along with a mathematical algorithm, is used to calculate the expected final temperature. In doing so, the measurement time is shortened from minutes to seconds.

Infrared clinical thermometers (IRETs) are 'non-contact' thermometers which sense the thermal radiation emitted in the infrared. An example of an infrared clinical thermometer is the tympanic (ear) thermometer. When inserted in the ear, a sensor inside the thermometer (either a thermopile or a pyroelectric detector) measures the thermal (infrared) radiation emitted by either the ear canal or the tympanic membrane, depending on the thermometer type. The temperature is shown on a digital display. Another example of an infrared thermometer is the temporal artery or 'forehead' thermometer, which is a non-invasive device designed to infer patient temperature by measuring the temperature of the temporal artery. Similar sensing elements to that of the tympanic thermometers are used.

Dot matrix (phase-change) thermometers use a series of chemicals which melt (changing phase from solid to liquid) at progressively higher temperatures. The sealed dots of material, each designed to melt at increments of 0.1 °C (32.2 °F), are arranged in a grid and sandwiched in a thin paper cover near the end of a card which is placed under the tongue.

Colour-change devices use liquid crystals that are manufactured as a flexible strip, which can then be applied to a surface such as the forehead. The temperature is indicated by the occurrence of colour changes in the

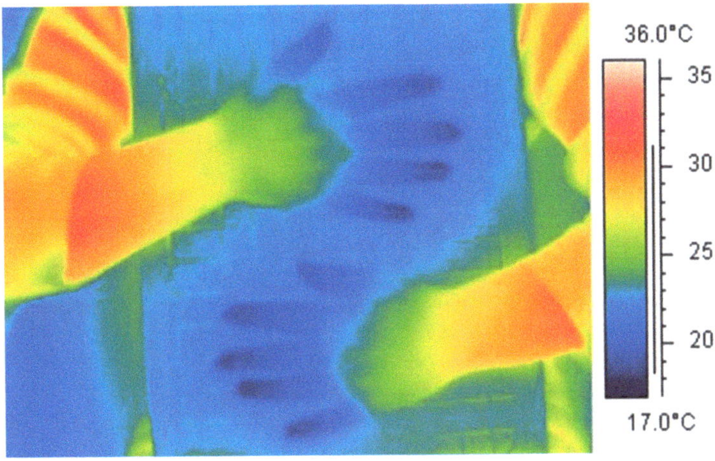

Fig. 4.3 Thermal imaging of the body with infrared thermometry. (With permission. © NPL Management Ltd., London, UK)

liquid crystals at the temperatures marked on the strip. For example, green may indicate 36 °C (96.8 °F), red 40 °C (104 °F), and so on. Many of these systems are reusable.

Thermography, or thermal imaging, is an extension of infrared thermometry. Measurements are made not just at one point, but over an extended area, resulting in an infrared photograph or video, or 'thermal image'. This image can be analysed to obtain a temperature map, using false colours to provide visual contrast between different temperatures. These systems are not commonly used, but many large clinical centres have such capability and they are implemented for specific conditional diagnosis, such as those linked to Raynaud's phenomenon (Fig. 4.3) [14].

Consider the role of thermography in the diagnosis of pain and inflammation.

Reflections

- Describe a thermometer that is accurate, patient safe, and not unpleasant for the individual.
- Reflect on the reliability of adjusting one site to another.
- Reflect on the pros and cons of different types of thermometers from a clinical perspective.

- Reflect on the acceptable variations in terms of stability and repeatability in clinical practice.
- Reflect on the concepts of technical and clinical accuracy.
- Consider what affects accuracy in a clinical situation.
- How do you calibrate electronic devices, such as rectal, oral, and axillary thermometers, in clinical practice?

References

1. IEC. Procès-Verbaux du Comité International des Poids et Mesures, 78th meeting. pp T1–T21 (French version) and pp T23–T42 (in English). Geneva: Electrotechnical Commission (IEC); 1989.
2. Quinn T. Temperature. 2nd ed. London: Academic Press; 1990.
3. Fraden J. Medical infrared thermometry (review of modern techniques). Temperature – its measurement & control in science & industry. 1992;6:825–30.
4. Simpson R, Machin G. Infrared ear thermometry: traceability and calibration at the National Physical Laboratory. IPEM ASM. 2003:150–1.
5. Simpson R, Machin G, McEvoy H, Fusby R. Traceability and calibration in temperature measurement: a clinical necessity. J Med Eng Technol. 2006;30 (4):212–7.
6. Ishii J, Fikuzaki T, McEvoy H, Simpson R, Machin G. A comparison of the blackbody cavities for infrared thermometers of NMIJ, NPL, and PTB. 9th international symposium on temperature and thermal measurements in industry and science; Dubrovnik: Tempmeko; 2004.
7. McEvoy H, Simpson R, Machin G. New blackbody standard for the evaluation and calibration of tympanic ear thermometers at the NPL, United Kingdom. In: Burleigh Dea, editor. Thermosence XXVI proceedings of the SPIE. 5405; np: 20042004. p. 56–60.
8. ISO/IECI. General requirements for the competence of testing and calibration laboratories ISO/IECI 17025. Geneva: International Organization for Standardization; 1999.
9. ASTME. ASTME 1965–98 (US) Standard specification for infrared thermometers for intermittent determination of patient temperature. 2009.
10. EN. Clinical thermometers. 2009.
11. JIS. Infrared Ear Thermometers. First publ. 25 March 2005, confirmed 25 October 2014. 4207 JIS T 4207 (Japan) http://engineers.ihs.com/document/abstract/TCHVHBAAAAAAAAAA.2014
12. Mackechnie C, Simpson R. Traceable calibration for blood pressure and temperature monitoring. Nurs Stand. 2006;26(11):42–7.
13. Crawford D, Wentworth S. Thermometer review 2005.
14. Ring F. Reynaud's phenomenon: assessment by thermography. Thermology. 1988;3:69–73.

CHAPTER 5

Thermoregulation of the Human Body

The body is an open system that needs to protect its internal environment from its surroundings. At the same time it is dependent on its surroundings for the exchange of oxygen, nutrients, waste products, and heat. These conflicting demands need particularly physiological mechanisms to maintain a stable and balanced internal environment, so-called homeostasis. The complex physiological self-regulatory mechanisms and processes required to achieve homeostasis are maintained by specialized organs and organ systems in the body. The ability to regulate and exchange body heat is essential for survival in humans. Regulation of body temperature operates via a neural feedback system. Sensory inflows indicating cold or heat from several different parts of the body, such as the skin and internal organs, reach specialized neurons located in the central nervous system, chiefly in the hypothalamus. The hypothalamus integrates the incoming sensory information and transmits neural and hormonal signals, initiating various kinds of physiological activity. The physiological activities represent, in broad terms, heat gain, or, alternatively, heat loss, and thus maintain an appropriate body temperature. Organs or organ systems besides the nervous system that are the main actors in regulation of body temperature are the cardiovascular system, the sudomotor control system, and skeletal muscles. These systems ensure that the rate of heat loss is balanced by the amount of heat gain so as to ensure an appropriate body temperature. Body temperature is regulated between fairly narrow limits: 35 °C

E. Grodzinsky, M. Sund Levander (eds.), *Understanding Fever and Body Temperature*, https://doi.org/10.1007/978-3-030-21886-7_5

(95 °F) to 41 °C (105.8 °F) [1]. An immoderate rise in body temperature (hyperthermia or hyperpyrexia) in which temperature regulation no longer works needs to be treated as a medical emergency.

Heat Production and Heat Loss

The human body produces heat continuously as a result of cell metabolism. During cell metabolism (cellular respiration), biochemical energy (from carbohydrates, fats, and proteins) is converted into chemical energy like adenosine triphosphate (ATP) and thermal energy. ATP is the form of energy that the cell mostly uses to drive various intracellular activities, for example, coupling actin and myosin in skeletal muscle contraction. The thermal energy, produced during cellular respiration, when exchanged with the surrondings, is called heat. In the body, heat will to some amount be stored and this is what we in everyday speech call body temperature. Body temperature in humans is ideally around 36 °C (96.8 °F) to 37 °C (98.6 °F), with a variation from approximately 33.4 °C (92.1 °F) to 38.2 °C (100.8 °F) depending on the site of measurement and the time of day [2]. In order to maintain a constant internal-deep-body temperature, heat loss must match heat gain.

In the resting state, most of the heat production originates from internal organs (~50%) and the remainder comes from the skeletal muscles, skin, brain, and skeleton. When engaged in physical activity, the skeletal muscles may contribute up to 90% of the total heat production. The body's ability to store heat is limited, and heat storage in connection with physical activity can be a challenge. On performing exercise at a relatively high intensity, for example, when jogging, the body temperature can rise to 38 °C (100.4 °F) in 10–20 minutes. This confirms the fact that the ability to regulate body temperature is essential for survival. The heat produced in the cells is absorbed into the blood and transported to the skin, where exchange of thermal energy between the blood and the surroundings can take place. This exchange, or heat flow, is known as thermodynamics [3].

Heat Transfer

As mentioned above, humans are an open system. This includes the fact that the body constantly exchanges energy with its surroundings. Exchange of heat can take place via four different physical mechanisms: radiation, conduction, convection, and evaporation (Fig. 5.1).

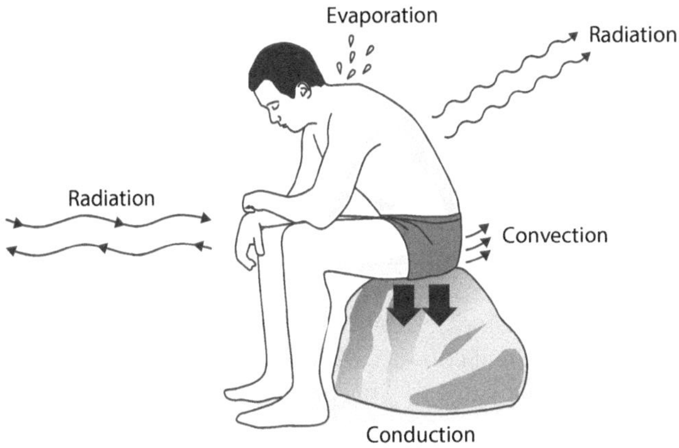

Fig. 5.1 Mechanisms of heat loss from the body. The amount of heat transferred from a body to the surrounding depends on, for example, ambient temperature, wetness, body size and composition, age, clothing, nutrition, and further circumstances like illness, injury, and pharmaceutical or drug use. The cooling rate is difficult to predict since the process of cooling involves many biological parameters. (With permission from illustrator Jonny Hallberg, Sjöbo Sweden)

Radiation, conduction, and convection are called dry heat exchange and evaporation is known as wet heat exchange. All of these, except radiation, need some kind of transporting medium—a gas, a fluid, or solid matter—to transfer the heat. The effectiveness of heat transfer via these mechanisms is mainly dependent on differences in temperature (thermal gradients), surface area, and humidity (water vapour pressure).

Radiation

Radiation involves the transport of heat by electromagnetic waves (photons) from a warmer subject to a colder one. If the body is surrounded by a colder environment or object, heat will be transferred from the body to the colder object. Approximately 60% of the heat loss from a naked individual at an ambient temperature of 21 °C (69.8 °F) occurs through radiation. The opposite occurs when the body absorbs heat, such as from sun rays, an open fire, or a heater. At an ambient temperature of 40 °C (105.8 °F), about 80% of the heat transferred from the warmer environment to the body is due to radiation [4]. Heat exchange by radiation is affected by absorption by the skin or a layer of clothing. Heat transfer by radiation does not require any kind of transporting medium. This means, for example, that exchange by radiation occurs without any physical contact.

Conduction

Conduction is a form of heat transport which requires physical contact with an object. The heat exchanged is determined by the area of the contact surface and the material's ability to transfer heat, that is, its thermal conductivity. The thermal conductivity of still air and water is about 0.026 and 0.6 Wm^{-1} K^{-1}, respectively. This means that the conductivity of water is about 25 times greater than still air. The difference in heat transport may be considerably larger, however, depending on the contact area and temperature difference.

Convection

Heat exchange by convection occurs when a gas or liquid flows past the surface of the skin. The amount of heat transported depends partly on the temperature differences between the skin and the ambient air and partly on the movement of air around the skin surface. Skin temperature varies, but in comfortable conditions it is around 30 °C (86 °F). When the surrounding air has a lower temperature, heat at the skin surface will be transferred to the surrounding air. The heated air is transported away, with the result that the temperature difference between the skin and the surrounding air increases once again and more heat can be conveyed from the skin to the air. The greatest temperature changes occur in a very thin layer closest to the surface of the skin. If the velocity of the air is increased, such as with a fan, the thin warm layer of air in contact with the skin will blow away, leading to a significant increase in heat exchange (wind chill factor) when the surrounding air temperature is lower than the skin temperature.

Reversibly, convectional heat exchange from the surroundings to the body occurs when the air temperature is above the skin temperature, for example, in a sauna with an air temperature of 80 °C (176 °F). Using a fan in a sauna would cause extreme pain and burn the skin. Even in an environment with less extreme heat, such as on a hot summer's day with a room temperature around 40 °C (104 °F), heat exchange from the surrounding air to the body will occur if a fan is being used. In addition to the importance of the surface area, the heat transfer coefficient also affects the amount of heat exchanged. For example, heat transferred by natural convection in water may be 100 times higher than that in air, and if the water is moving at, say, 5 m/s, heat lost by convection is 5000 times higher.

What is the point of layering clothing?
What is the point of wearing a hat on a sunny day?

Evaporation

Evaporation occurs when a substance is transformed from a liquid to a gas. This transformation requires energy in the form of heat, for example. When warm blood reaches the surface of the skin, heat will be transferred from the blood to the skin. At the surface of the skin, sweat molecules, secreted by sweat glands, will absorb thermal energy and evaporate into the surrounding air. In environments with a temperature higher than the skin temperature, evaporation is the only form of heat transfer that can cool the body. The higher the ambient humidity, the more difficult this process of removing heat from the body by evaporating sweat molecules. As the ambient humidity approaches 100% (e.g., in a tropical forest) and the air temperature approaches skin temperature, the difference in partial vapour pressure between the ambient air and the skin decreases. Sweat flows off the body instead of being evaporated and heat transport decreases. When humidity and air temperature exceed skin temperature, condensation occurs in which water molecules with excess energy from the ambient air will land onto the skin surface. Most people cannot tolerate prolonged ambient temperatures above around 33 °C (91.4 °F) if combined with high humidity, even when resting. At higher ambient temperatures the body will absorb heat through radiation, convection, and conduction, and the risk of overheating is severe.

Heat Balance

To attain a body temperature within the normal range it is necessary to maintain heat balance. This is achieved when the amount of heat produced in the body and the amount of heat leaving or being transferred to the body is in balance. In a cold surrounding, storage of heat will be the primary concern, while a warm surrounding leads to heat leaving the body. Under normal circumstances, heat balance is maintained by physiological effects and behaviour. In ambient air with a temperature of 20 °C (68 °F) with no wind, a human body will lose heat to the surrounding air mainly by radiation (~60%) and convection (~40%). Evaporation represents only a very minimal part of the total. If the ambient temperature rises to 30 °C (86 °F), radiation and convection represent around 30% and 15%, respectively, while evaporation becomes the most important (around 55%). With an ambient air temperature of 40 °C (104 °F), evaporation becomes the only way to remove heat from the body, assuming humidity is not too high [4, 5].

Physiology of Thermoregulation

Thermoreceptors

There are several parts of the central nervous system involved in body temperature regulation. One of the major contributors is the hypothalamus, and a specific region called the preoptic area of the anterior hypothalamus (POAH), which is considered to be the main centre for temperature control. POAH contains neurons which sense the local temperature and integrate it with afferent thermal information. The local temperature is recorded in the blood that passes by the hypothalamus. Afferent temperature information arrives from remote thermoreceptors, mainly located in the skin, spinal cord, mucosa, and visceral areas. The integration allows selective thermoregulatory response, suitable for both internal and external temperature conditions (Fig. 5.2) [6].

Thermosensitive neurons in the POAH area respond not only to temperature but also to non-thermal stimuli. For example, various endogen substances, such as interleukin (IL)-1 and prostaglandin E, are mediators involved in immunological responses which can initiate 'fever' (see Chap. 6). These neurons also respond to stimuli such as motion sickness, seasickness, hormones (testosterone, oestrogen, and progesterone), and levels of glucose and electrolytes (osmolality) in the blood. Cold-sensitive neurons decrease their sensitivity at low glucose levels and increase their sensitivity at elevated osmolality [6]. Motion sickness weakens the vasoconstrictor response to the skin, leading to increased heat loss. This may predispose seasick individuals to hypothermia in conjunction with cold water immersion [7]. That 'non-thermal factors' affect the neuronal network in the POAH area is an indication that there is interaction between homeostatic

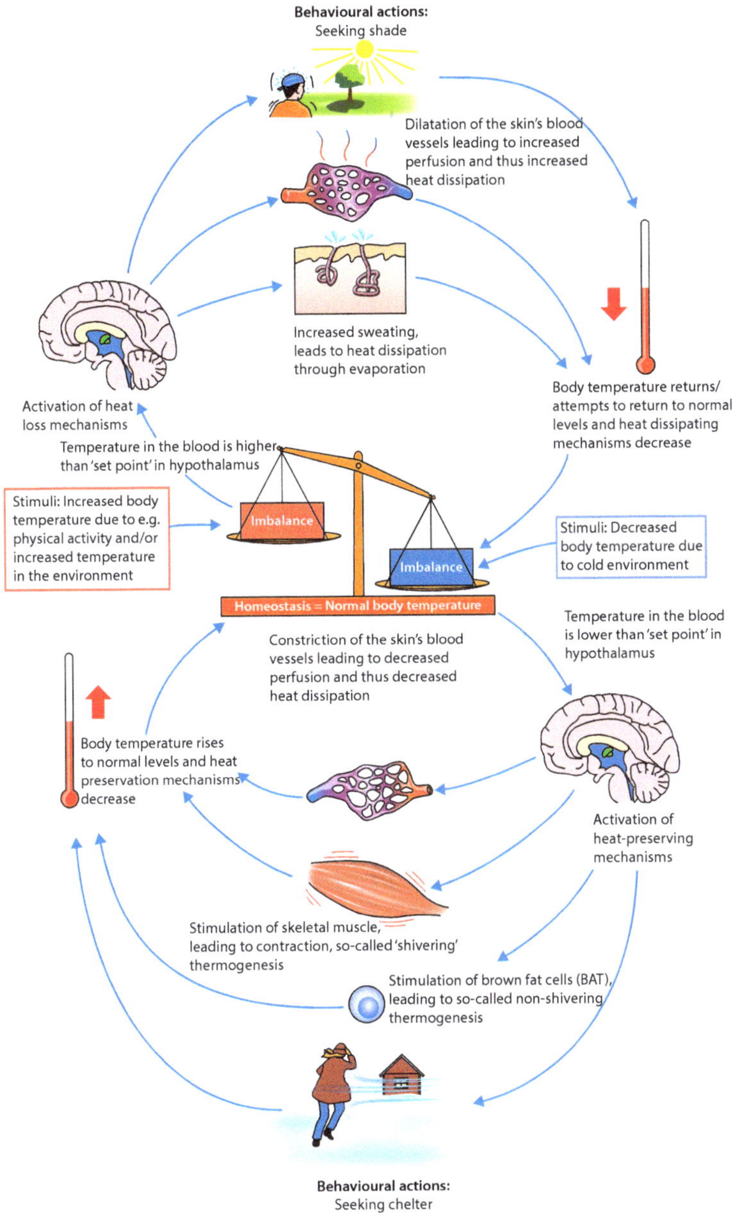

Fig. 5.2 Schematic view of regulation of body temperature. Heat balance is maintained by physiological and behavioural actions. (With permission from illustrator Jonny Hallberg, Sjöbo Sweden)

systems. These 'non-temperature factors' which change in relation to season, light, and diet are probably the explanation for temperature-related adaptation [6, 7].

Afferent temperature signals are generated both in the skin and in other key areas of the body [6, 8]. The skin's role in temperature regulation is of great importance. All temperature responses, both physiological and behaviour-related, are largely based on input from the skin [9]. The skin has sensory nerve endings with particular receptors sensitive to temperature.

These receptors, which belong to the transient receptor potential (TRP) family, have a certain type of ion channels in their cell membrane which respond to a wide range of different temperatures. Some receptors are nociceptive and bring about the sensation of pain when stimulated with high temperatures (above 42 °C; 107.6 °F) or low temperatures (below 18 °C; 64.4 °F) [8]. Other receptors pass on information concerning temperatures that range within the interval where there is no risk of tissue damage or any larger threats to the maintenance of normal body temperature. In addition to temperature, other non-thermal stimuli may influence these receptors. One example is capsaicin, found in chilli peppers, a substance that both activates (feels hot) and increases sensitivity to thermal stimuli [10]. Receptors that detect colder temperatures also react to substances such as menthol and wasabi (Japanese horseradish). Other non-thermal factors that activate these receptors include substances produced during inflammation (e.g., acetylcholine, ATP, cytokines).

It is unknown if thermal sensitivity is uniform in all areas of the skin. The temperature sensitivity of the face seems to be four to five times higher than the sensitivity of the limbs. An increase in skin temperature of the facial skin by 4 °C (39.2 °F) results in an increase in general sweating by about 50%. Rapid cooling of the facial skin gives a response that is two to five times stronger in terms of reduced generalized sweating compared to the rapid cooling of the extremities. Research has also shown that the torso, compared to the extremities, has a larger thermal sensitivity [11], and that sensitive receptors are to a greater extent located at the forearms, hands, lower legs, feet, and head [12, 13].

How to cool yourself in a hot environment without access to a bath or shower?

Set Point or Thermoeffector Threshold Zone

The classical explanatory model of temperature regulation and the centrally located hypothalamus is the 'set point' concept. This explanatory model considers the hypothalamus to function like a thermostat, comparing incoming temperature information with a reference temperature. Any temperature deviations result in an 'error signal', with subsequent appropriate autonomous reactions, such as a change in vasomotor tone, sweating, or shivering. This type of control and regulation is called a negative feedback control system. Another, more recent, didactic model is the 'thermoeffector threshold zone'. This model describes a temperature zone where neither sweating nor muscle contraction occurs. Variations in the body's internal temperature within this 'temperature window' are adjusted only through variations in the blood flow in the skin. Non-thermal factors such as sleep, nausea, osmolarity, and nitrous oxide also impinge on the thermoregulatory system [5]. This model, in contrast to the classical 'set point' model, makes it possible to include non-thermal factors and their impact on thermoregulation.

How to Maintain Normal Body Temperature

To maintain an internal-deep-body temperature within a normal range is crucial for the body since many physiological processes are at their optimum within a very narrow range of body temperatures. Heat balance is, under normal circumstances, maintained by behaviour and physiological reactions. Behaviour plays a very important role, especially when ambient temperature reaches outside the thermoneutral zone (TNZ), when regulatory changes in either heat production or heat loss are needed. To adjust the rates of heat loss and heat gain, humans use a variety of behaviours. For example, appropriate actions include seeking the shade, avoiding wind and wetness, increasing or decreasing physical activity, and wearing suitable clothing [14]. Physiological reactions involve the cardiovascular system, the sudomotor control, and metabolism.

Cardiovascular System

A vital part of the body's temperature regulation is changes in skin blood flow. Regulation of body temperature is primarily controlled through changes to blood perfusion by vasodilatation or vasoconstriction in subcutaneous blood vessels. In a resting state and with a thermoneutral surrounding, skin blood flow represents approximately 5% of cardiac output, which is about 0.3 litre/min. When heat gain is increased, as in physical activity in hot ambient temperatures, skin blood flow can increase up to 60% of the increased cardiac output, that is, about 8 litre/min [15, 16]. However, these increased physiological demands require a strong and healthy heart and circulatory system. The most common vascular construction in the skin is arteries coupled to veins via capillaries. Fewer in number are the direct artery-vein connections, the so-called arterial venous anastomoses. These are mainly found in the skin of acral areas like the hands and fingers, feet and toes, nose, lips, cheeks, and ears. When the blood flows through artery to venous anastomoses, the heat loss is less substantial than when passing through capillaries [9].

Vasomotor activity (vasoconstriction or vasodilatation) is chiefly controlled by the sympathetic nervous system. Vasoconstriction is mainly controlled via the transmitter substance noradrenalin and the adrenergic receptors $\alpha 1$ and $\alpha 2$. The pathways of signal transmission for vasodilation are not yet fully understood. One hypothesis is that active vasodilation is achieved by acetylcholine-mediated nitric oxide (NO) release [16, 17]. Some part of the vasomotor activity in the skin is also affected by local substances such as prostaglandins and neurotransmitters like neuropeptide Y (NPY) from sensory nerve endings. The venous part of the skin circulation participates by reducing tonus when heat loss is needed, especially in the veins below the heart level. Estimated pooled volumes are 300–500 ml, which can have an impact on central venous return and thereby stroke volume [9].

Sudomotor Control

Evaporation of sweat via sweat glands in the skin occurs more or less appreciably at all times. Humans have about two to five million eccrine sweat glands, with the highest density in areas such as the palms of the hands and the soles of the feet. Sweat glands are activated via sympathetic nerves, with signals originating in the hypothalamus. The chief neurotransmitter is acetylcholine, but adrenergic substances also have a certain influence. This rather unusual sympathetic cholinergic neural mix is said to be developed directly after birth by mechanisms which are as yet unknown. The amount of sweat that is secreted and its sodium content varies according to several different factors, such as the number of activated sweat glands and their capacity. This also depends on the individual's aerobic capacity, whether they are well adapted to elevated body temperatures, their age, and genetic factors. During hard physical labour, evaporation can increase significantly, and sweat production may reach 1.5 litres/hour in an unfit individual, and more than 5 litres/hour for those trained in endurance. However, evaporative endurance is limited, so after a few hours of profuse sweating, intensity will be reduced [4]. Evaporation is a very important mechanism to maintain normal body temperature when the ambient temperature rises to approach body temperature. With a surrounding temperature of 40 °C (104 °F), evaporation is the only way to exchange heat between the body and its surroundings. Evaporation counteracts overheating, particularly during physical work.

Metabolism

As mentioned earlier, a large amount of heat is produced in connection with muscle contractions. Shivering, or shivering thermogenesis, consists of involuntary muscle contractions initiated via temperature stimuli, primarily from the core and secondarily from the skin. However, the intensity of shivering is based on the integration of temperature information, and rapid changes in skin temperature can have serious effects on shivering response. Other factors that can influence shivering intensity are blood glucose, as well as the intramuscular and intrahepatic glycogen layer. Low blood glucose seems to influence the neurons in the hypothalamus' ability to intergrade ingoing and outgoing temperature-related traffic. The glycogen layer may affect the ability to produce muscle contraction, although lipid metabolism is a good source when the glycogen layer is depleted. Shivering can occur at different intensity levels and can indeed consume large amounts of energy, that is, up to five or six times the metabolic rate in resting muscle. The intensity of shivering increases with increased demands for heat production. Shivering in the early stages is not apparent to the human eye. Shivering thermogenesis begins with ambient air temperatures or water temperatures of 23 °C (73.4 °F) to 26 °C (78.8 °F) or when the gradient between the core and peripheral temperature increases too much. Shivering is a rather complex physiological phenomenon, involving many different structures and pathways in the central nervous system. Neurons that induce or suppress shivering are, for example, located in different nuclei of the basal ganglia, hypothalamus, pons, medulla oblongata, and spinal cord. Three of the neurotransmitters involved are noradrenalin, acetylcholine, and serotonin.

Non-shivering thermogenesis takes place in brown adipose tissue (BAT) and is important for thermoregulation in newborns and some animals, such as rodents. Non-shivering thermogenesis in BAT is probably also involved in the thermogenesis of healthy adults. Adipocytes in BAT withhold a great number of mitochondria that have a certain ability to produce energy in the form of heat, especially using lipids. BAT thermogenesis is activated via the sympathetic nervous system using norepinephrine and β adrenergic receptors.

What is the purpose of shivering thermogenesis?

Factors Affecting Body Temperature

So far we have focused on the hypothalamic control and regulation of body temperature via feedback from thermosensitive tissue, resulting in changes in blood flow, sweating, and metabolism—the so-called thermal factors. Yet, just as with the hypothalamus, these thermal factors can be influenced by other non-thermal factors. Non-thermal factors can either increase or decrease the hypothalamic sensitivity and threshold, and thereby affect responses associated with body temperature regulation. Non-thermal factors include various pharmacological agents, endogen substances such as cytokines and prostaglandins (e.g., IL-1 and E2 that are involved in the fever response, see Chap. 6) and hormones (e.g., in the ovarian cycle), plasma osmolality and volume, and exercise [4].

Another non-thermal factor which can affect body temperature without directly involving the hypothalamus is thyroid hormone (thyroxine). Thyroid hormone exerts a direct influence on cellular metabolism by stimulating a number of different intracellular energy-consuming events such as Na^+/K^+ ATPase activity (sodium/potassium pumps) and increased number of β receptors. Hormone overproduction increases the number of sodium/potassium pump and β receptors (increased activity in the sympathetic nervous system) which leads to increased energy production, and thus increased heat production and elevated body temperature. An increase in metabolism is achieved by thyroid hormone through gene transcription and takes weeks to attain [18]. A lower hormone production will have the opposite effect. Increased metabolism is also associated with increased physical activity and, as previously mentioned, intense muscle work can elevate body temperature by 1 °C (33.8 °F) within

10–20 minutes. The factors which directly increase the metabolism of the cells are usually called chemical thermogenesis [4].

An immoderate rise in body temperature (hyperthermia or hyperpyrexia) in which temperature regulation no longer works needs to be treated as a medical emergency. Heat illness is characterized by three different stages, where symptoms such as muscle cramps, nausea, reduced cognitive ability, low blood pressure, reduced sweating, and reduced consciousness accelerate as the body becomes warmer. When body temperature is around 40 °C (104 °F), heat stroke is diagnosed, which is the most severe stage of heat illness. In this stage, the absence of sweating is an important diagnostic sign and vital parameters are severely affected. If not treated, multiple organ failure may develop due to the denaturation of proteins, deranged coagulation, rhabdomyolysis, and haemorrhages in the skin and intestines. It is essential for good prognosis, and even survival, that the whole body is cooled very rapidly. An important fact is that the ability to withstand heat illness varies considerably among the population due to a large number of factors [3, 6] (see Chaps. 6 and 7).

Age and Gender Differences

The youngest and the oldest members of healthy population have an increased risk of developing both hypothermia and hyperthermia. Maturation and age-related degeneration play an important role in modifying thermoregulatory responses to temperature challenges. The absolute youngest (neonates) have a not yet fully developed thermoregulation and rely on heat production via non-shivering thermogenesis (BAT). Younger people also have a greater surface area relative to their mass, which means that loss of body heat in cold surroundings is more rapid than that in adults. When it comes to the behavioural aspects of thermoregulation, maturity level may also differ with regard to age.

The elderly are more vulnerable since the capacity of the nervous system is more or less reduced due to age-related degeneration. This means that older adults have reduced physical and behavioural responses to thermal challenges. This fact is evident in the way that the elderly are clearly overrepresented in connection with heat-related illness and death. Heat stress involves an increased workload for the heart, changes in vascular tonus, and sweating, which are all largely regulated by the autonomic nervous system [16, 19]. A rise in body temperature from 36.5 °C (97.9 °F) to 39 °C (102.2 °F) increases the workload on the heart by around 50% [20]. Sensitivity, transmission, and integration in the neurons involved in temperature-related information may also be reduced, both peripherally and centrally [21, 22]. When it comes to cold stress, older adults have a reduced ability to vasoconstrict and to produce heat by shivering, and in general they have less subcutaneous adipose tissue, and therefore have reduced insulation and less metabolic substrate available. Cold ambient temperatures lead to a higher incident of coronary and cerebral thrombosis probably due to changes in blood pressure and blood viscosity.

The interthreshold zone in elderly adults is broader than in other adults. This means that thermoregulatory responses such as shivering and sweating are initiated at lower and higher body temperatures, respectively. This, in combination with reduced physical and behavioural responses to thermal challenge, puts the elderly at risk of developing hypothermia and hyperthermia due to endogenous or exogenous thermal stress [23]. During the progress of menopause, oestrogen levels fluctuate and decline. This can affect thermoregulation in several ways like, for example, hypothalamic response to neurotransmitters (serotonin and norepinephrine) involved in the thermoregulation and vascular reactivity. This means, in simple terms, that 'set point' or TNZ may be slightly more sensitive to changes in core body temperature and that the communication with skin blood vessels and endocrine glands are less functional. This disturbance may cause hot flashes (increased skin temperature and sweating) in conjunction with increased core temperature [17, 24].

Alterations in Body Temperature: Hyperthermia and Hypothermia

Hyperthermia, or heat stroke, can be categorized into two forms—classical and exertional. The former usually occurs among the elderly, the chronically ill, the physical or mentally disabled, and young children, whereas the latter mostly affects military and rescue personnel and athletes. Besides high ambient temperature and humidity, risk factors include circulatory and respiratory diseases, as well as the use of some medicines (e.g., antipyretics, beta blockers, diuretics, psychoactive drugs, antidepressants, anticholinergics, antihistamines, and antiepileptic drugs) [25]. Some other risk factors are obesity, skin defects, neurological disease, drugs, dehydration, infection, and physical activity. Yet another risk is the inability to adjust to environmental temperature, for example, when a sleeping child is confined in a heated car or left sleeping outdoors in the summertime while dressed in too many clothes. In these cases there is a risk of excessive heat conservation that exceeds the heat dissipation capacity [26]. Hyperthermia is a condition when the body temperature is so high that there is a risk of damaged cell proteins, as well as disturbed or even non-functioning thermoregulation [18]. Hyperthermia is a life-threatening condition that requires immediate action in the form of active cooling until thermoregulation is normalized [27]. Treatment in hyperthermia is based on principles for heat dissipation with radiation, convection, and evaporation [25].

In the opposite case, when heat dissipation exceeds heat production, there is a risk of severely decreased body temperature, or hypothermia. Hypothermia is defined in five stages: mild from 32 °C (91.4 °F) to 34 °C (93.2 °F); moderate from 28 °C (82.4 °F) to 31.9 °C (89.4 °F); deep from 11 °C (51.8 °F) to 27.9 °C (82.2 °F); profound from 6 °C (42.8 °F) to 10.9 °C (51.6 °F); and ultra-profound below 6 °C (42.8 °F) [28]. Body temperatures below 35 °C (95 °F) carry the risk of impaired cardiac performance and muscle function, cerebral effects, and release of stress hormones. At 34 °C (93.2 °F), cellular metabolism and thermoregulatory functions cease. At 30 °C (86 °F), thermoregulation does not function at all [29]. Accidental causes of hypothermia are cooling in conjunction with trauma, ingestion of alcohol with subsequent loss of consciousness, or cooling in cold water or snow. In order to decrease metabolism, hypothermia can also be induced on purpose in specific surgical procedures (see Chap. 9).

Consider thermoregulation in a marathon runner running 42 km in 40 °C (104°F) heat.
What about a drunk falling asleep in a snowdrift?

Reflections

- Reflect on how to retain body heat in cold, windy weather.
- Reflect on material used for clothes in both cold and warm weather.
- Reflect on how thermoregulation influences your actions at various temperatures, including when feverish.

- Reflect on sudomotor control in different climates.
- Reflect on the instruction 'Put on your cap and gloves and wear warm shoes'.
- Reflect on how to promote heat loss in a warm, humid environment.

References

1. Pierau F. Peripheral thermosensors. In: Blatties CMaF, IMJ, editor. Environmental physiology, Handbook of physiology, vol. 1. Oxford: Oxford University Press; 1996.
2. Sund Levander M, Forsberg C, Wahren LK. Normal oral, rectal, tympanic and axillary body temperature in adult men and women: a systematic literature review. Scand J Caring Sci. 2002;16(2):122–8.
3. Taylor N, Groeller H. Physiological bases of human performance during work and exercise. Edinburgh: Churchill Livingstone; 2008.
4. Greger R, Windhorst U. Comprehensive human physiology: from cellular mechanism to integration. Berlin/Heidelberg: Springer; 1996.
5. Danielsson U. Convection coefficients in clothing air layers. Stockholm: The Royal Institute of Technology; 1993.
6. Boulant J. Hypothalamic neurons regulating body temperature. In: Blatties CaF, IMJ, editor. Environmental physiology, Handbook of physiology, vol. 1. Oxford: Oxford University Press; 1996.
7. Mekjavic I, Eiken O. Contribution of thermal and nonthermal factors to the regulation of body temperature in humans. J Appl Physiol. 2006;100:2065–72.
8. Catania A, Airaghi L, Motta P, Manfredi M, Annini G, Pettenati C, et al. Cytokine antagonists in aged subjects and their relation with cellular immunity. J Gerontol Biol Sci Med. 1997;52(2):B 93–7.
9. Jessen C, editor. Interaction of body temperatures in control of thermoregulatory effector mechanism. In Environmental physiology. Oxford: Oxford University Press; 1996.
10. Kah nS, Hull R. Utzschneider KM. Mechanisms linking obesity to insulin resistance and type 2 diabetes. Nature. 2006;444:840–6.
11. Cotter J, Taylor N. The distribution of cutaneous sudomotor and alliesthesial thermosensitivity in mildly heat stressed humans: an open loop approach. J Physiol. 2005;565(1):335–45.
12. Loke A, Chan H, Chan T. Comparing the effectiveness of two types of cooling blankets for febrile patients. Nurs Crit Care. 2005;10(5):247–54.
13. Sund Levander M, Wahren LK. Assessment and prevention of shivering in patients with severe cerebral injury. A pilot study. J Clin Nurs. 2000;9:55–61.
14. Taylor ME, Oppenheim BA. Hospital- acquired infection in elderly patients. J Hosp Infect. 1998;38:245–60.
15. Johnson M, Proppe W. Cardiovascular adjustment to heat stress Oxford: OUP, 1996. In: Blatties C, editor. Handbook of physiology: environmental physiology. New York: Oxford; 1996.

16. Kellog D Jr, Zhao J, Coey U, Green J. Nitric oxide concentrations increases in the cutaneous interstitial space during heat stress in human. J Appl Physiol. 2006;98(2):629–32.
17. Charkouidan N. Skin blood flow in adult human thermoregulation: how it works, when it does not, and why. Mayo Clin Proc. 2003;12(108):729–35.
18. Guyton A, Hall J. Body temperature, temperature regulation and fever. In: Guyton ACHJ, editor. Textbook of medical physiology. 13th ed. Philadelphia: W. B. Saunders Company; 2012. p. 822–33.
19. Ferrari A, Radaelli A, Centola M. Physiology of aging: aging and the cardiovascular system. J Appl Physiol. 2003;95:2591–7.
20. Deussen A. Hyperthermie und hypothermie (in German). Der Anaesthesist [Anaesthesist]. 2007;56(9):907–11.
21. Folklov B, Svanborg A. Physiology of cardiovascular ageing. Physiol Rev. 1993;74(4):724–64.
22. Munce T, Kenney W. Age-specific skin blood flow responses to acute capsaicin. J Gerontol A Biol Sci Med Sci. 2003;58(4):304–10.
23. Andersson GS, Meneilly GS, Makjavic LB. Passive temperature lability in the elderly. Eur J Appl Physiol. 1996;73(3–4):278–86.
24. Feedman R. Core body temperature variation in symptomatic and asymptomatic postmenopausal women: brief report. Menopause. 2002;9:399–401.
25. Bouchama A, Dehbi M, Chaves-Carballo E. Cooling and hemodynamic management in heatstroke: practical recommendations. Critical Care. 2007;11(R54(3)):1–10.
26. Axelrod P. External cooling in the management of fever. Clin Infect Dis. 2000;31(Suppl 5):S224–9.
27. Knochel JP, Goodman EL. Heat stroke and other forms of hyperthermia. Elevations in body temperature not mediated by endogenous pyrogens. In: Mackowi-ak PA, editor. Fever basic mechanisms and management. 2nd ed. Philadelphia/New York: Lippincott Raven; 1997. p. 437–57.
28. Varon J. Therapeutic hypothermia; implications for acute care practitioners. Postgrad Med. 2010;122:19–27.
29. Granberg PO. Human physiology under cold exposure. Arctic Med Res. 1991;50(suppl. 6):23–7;50, suppl. 6,:23–7

General References

Guyton A, Hall J. Body temperature, temperature regulation and fever. In: Guyton AC, Hall J, editors. Textbook of medical physiology. 13th ed. Philadelphia: W.B. Saunders; 2012.

Christensson R. Anatomi och fysiologi för sjuksköterskor [Anatomy and physiology for nurses]. Stockholm: Pearson Education; 2012.

CHAPTER 6

Physiological and Immunological Activity

Depending on one's point of view, immunology can be regarded as a very young or a very old medical specialty; one of the smallest or one of the largest; one of the simplest or one of the most complicated. Half a century ago, immunology was almost synonymous with infectious diseases and microbiology. The main purpose of our immune system is to protect us from infection of various kinds, but there are two sides to the immune system. When its dual nature was understood, immunology became a specialty in its own right, separate from the study of infectious diseases. Infection of cells by microorganisms activates an inflammatory response, which is a protective response by the body, ensuring removal of detrimental stimuli, as well as a healing process for repairing damaged tissue [1]. Classically, inflammation is characterized by five symptoms: redness, swelling, heat, pain, and loss of tissue function. These macroscopic symptoms reflect an increased permeability of the vascular endothelium, allowing leakage of serum components and immune cells. When pathogens or injuries threaten the body, two different branches of the immune system work together to restore homeostasis: the innate and the adaptive immune systems.

An increase in body temperature has been known for a very long time to be associated with 'something not is as it should be'. When we say that someone has a 'fever', what do we really mean? In the first place, most people think of fever as being the same as a disease and an elevated body temperature. However, fever is actually a part of a larger response in the body when many different cells are activated, in what is called the 'acute-phase response'.

E. Grodzinsky, M. Sund Levander (eds.), *Understanding Fever and Body Temperature*, https://doi.org/10.1007/978-3-030-21886-7_6

When pathogens or injuries threaten the body, two different branches of the immune system work together to restore homeostasis: these are the innate and the adaptive immune systems. These two branches provide either immediate protection with broad specificity or delayed and prolonged protection with exquisite specificity. The numerous pathogens we encounter on a daily basis do not normally cause disease because most are quickly eliminated by the innate immune system.

Cytokines are small functional proteins involved in the immune response to infection or injury. Cytokines play essential roles in shaping an immune response to foreign or self-antigens. The cytokines which are released by tissues in the earliest phase of infection are members of a family of chemoattractant cytokines and are named chemokines. The stimulated cells undergo changes in cell adhesiveness, and in the cytoskeleton, resulting in a directed migration of the cell. Chemokines can be produced and released by many different cell types in response to bacterial products, viruses, and agents that cause physical damage. In the immune system, they mainly affect leukocytes, recruiting effector cells from the bloodstream onto the sites of infection. The interaction between pathogen recognition, tissue damage, and released mediators initiates an inflammatory response. Cytokines affect nearly every biological process, including embryonic development, disease pathogenesis, non-specific responses to infection, specific responses to antigens, changes in cognitive function, and the progression of the degenerative aging process.

The cytokines are subdivided into a number of large families and are classified on the basis of their biological activity as pro-inflammatory (Interleukin-1 family) or anti-inflammatory (Interleukin-10 family). Some cytokines are described in more detail below. In addition, cytokines play an important role in stem cell differentiation, vaccine efficacy, and allograft rejection. However, the two branches of pro- and anti-inflammatory cytokines must effectively coordinate a response in order to prevent inflammation or to target it in an appropriate way. The name interleukin (IL) refers to molecules secreted by, or acting on leukocytes. Some cytokines, such as IL-1, IL-6, and tumor necrosis factor (TNF), act in a broad manner to provoke an inflammatory response and induce the acute-phase response of the liver, including increased body temperature.

The acute-phase response is an early set of inflammatory reactions in endothermic animals comprising non-specific biochemical and biophysical responses, which are initiated by microbes or tissue degradation such as burns, trauma, and neoplasia. In humans, there is an increased hepatic production and a release of proteins into the blood stream in response to pro-inflammatory cytokines produced by macrophages and dendritic cells. These cytokines have local effects, and also long-range effects such as elevation of body temperature, and are mainly the endogenous pyrogens TNF-α, IL-1β, and IL-6. The proteins which are synthesized and released into the blood are called acute-phase proteins. These include C-reactive protein (CRP), mannose-binding lectin (MBL), serum amyloid A (SAA), fibrinogen, haptoglobin, α1-antitrypsin, α2-macroglobulin, α1-acid glycoprotein, and ferritin, and are described in more detail below. At the same time, other proteins, such as albumin and transferrin, the iron transport proteins, are reduced [2]. Although the acute-phase response is important for the immune response and has a rapid onset, it can be persistent in chronic inflammation and thus cause tissue destruction (see Chap. 8).

What actually happens when you catch a cold?

Physiological and Immunological Function of the Immune System

Inflammation is group of processes which are involved when homeostasis in tissues is disturbed as a result of an acute or chronic stimulus from an infection, stress, autoimmune reaction, or mechanical injury. Hemostasis is one of these processes and stops bleeding, retaining blood within the damaged blood vessel. This is the first stage of wound healing, and most of the time, it involves blood changing from a liquid to a solid state. Intact blood vessels are central to moderating the tendency of the blood to clot. This can be important in preventing a pathogen from entering the blood stream and spreading through the blood to organs throughout the body, causing sepsis. The homeostatic immune response is mainly mediated by polymorphonuclear leucocytes (PMN), with the disturbance depending on the balance of the cytokine profile [3]. Both macrophages and neutrophils secrete mediators such as prostaglandins, leukotrienes, and platelet-activating factor (PAF).

An inflammatory response is usually initiated within hours of infection, trauma, or wounding. Macrophages are stimulated to secrete pro-inflammatory cytokines and chemokines by interactions between microbes and microbial products and specific receptors expressed by the macrophages. Immune responses involve a rapid production of pro-inflammatory cytokines, which serve to initiate the host's defense against pathogens and cellular damage. Excessive inflammation may give rise to disturbances which are harmful to the host organism. Anti-inflammatory cytokines react so as to regulate the inflammatory process, limiting tissue damage and restoring homeostasis. Neutrophils, which are rapidly recruited to inflammatory sites, are responsible for dampening the inflammatory response [4].

The non-specific immune system, the innate system, is designed to give immediate protection on the first occasion the body meets any foreign or potentially infective agents. There are certain factors which affect the defense mechanism. The innate system uses a variety of pattern recognition receptors that may be expressed on the cell surface, in intracellular compartments, or secreted into the bloodstream and tissue fluids, and which include the pathogen-associated molecular patterns (PAMPs). The first line of defense against microorganisms is the physical barrier provided by the skin and the mucous membranes. The body enhances its defense by certain physiological factors, such as the hydrochloric acid in the stomach, the ciliated epithelium in the respiratory tract, the flushing action of urine in the urinary tract, the large amount of unsaturated fatty acids found in the skin, the enzyme lysozyme found in human tears and saliva, and the normal flora found on the skin and in the gut.

The innate system is responsible for the inflammatory responses triggered by many cells, such as white blood cells which are not B cells or T cells of the adaptive system. Among the cells that bear innate immune or germline-encoded recognition receptors are macrophages, dendritic cells (DCs), mast cells, neutrophils, eosinophils, and the natural killer cells (NK cells), which are described in more detail below. The second line of defense is stimulated if the invading organism or agent breaks through the first line—the inflammatory response and phagocytosis. If the innate system is unable to deal with an infection, activation of the adaptive system becomes necessary. The innate system can instruct the adaptive system as to the nature of the pathogen through the expression of co-stimulatory molecules, such as CD80 and CD86 [5]. After four to seven days, the adaptive system, also called the specific immune system, responds. The innate and adaptive systems are closely integrated during the different stages of an immune response. At each encounter with an antigen, the challenge for the immune system is to choose the correct type of effector mechanism in order to effectively eliminate foreign agents, and at the same time, protect the body from immune-mediated tissue damage. The T and B cells of the adaptive system have receptors which need to be assembled from gene segments, which allow great variability in adaptive immune recognition. Viruses, and some bacterial pathogens, can gain access to the intracellular compartments, such as the cytosol. Several pattern recognition receptors are expressed in the cytosol, where these intracellular pathogens are detected, and a response is induced that blocks their replication.

Innate immunity is primarily dedicated to taking care of the post-injury response, while in the post-infection stage the innate and the adaptive systems are integrated. When danger is detected, anti-inflammatory and pro-inflammatory factors are stimulated to repair injured tissue and to eliminate any infection in such a way as to minimize local cellular damage [6]. There is a cellular response from phagocytes and DCs and a humoral response in the form of acute-phase proteins, cytokines, the complement system, and leukotrienes [7].

The adaptive immune system also enables the unfortunate effects of autoimmune diseases, allergies, and allograft rejections, which are all responses to non-pathogen antigens. One of the advantages of the adaptive system is the ability to remember or adapt to an infectious agent. This is on an individual basis—it is developed during the lifetime of a specific individual and depends upon the foreign agents that an individual comes into contact with is associated with a decline in immune function known as immunosenescence, comprising an increase in cytokine release and a decline in the anti-inflammatory feedback system [8]. The balance between pro-inflammatory cytokines and anti-inflammatory cytokines changes with age. It has been suggested that changes in the lymphocyte subsets, such as an increase in CD 8+ T cells, are predictive of mortality [9].

Inflammatory Activity Within Infections

The principal physiological function of the immune system is to protect the host against pathogenic microbes. The evolution of an infectious disease in an individual involves a sequence of interactions between the microbe and the host. Some microbes produce disease by liberating toxins. Many of the characteristics of microorganisms help to determine their virulence, and a wide range of diverse mechanisms contribute to the pathogenesis of the infectious diseases they cause.

Extracellular microbes are rapidly killed by the principal mechanism of natural immunity: the phagocytes, neutrophils, monocytes, and macrophages. Endotoxins stimulate the production of cytokines by macrophages and other cells. The principal physiological function of macrophage-derived cytokines is to stimulate inflammation. These cytokines induce the adhesion of phagocytic cells, followed by migration and activation of inflammatory cells.

Cytokines induce an increase in body temperature and stimulate the synthesis of acute-phase proteins. They may also stimulate the mechanism for specific immunity, where the principal mechanism is the humoral immune system. Some of the most immunogenic components of the cell walls of microbes are polysaccharides. Such antigens directly stimulate B cells and the production of a strong specific Immunoglobulin (Ig) M response (primary immune response). In addition, other Ig isotypes may be produced as a result of the production of cytokines, which promote heavy chain isotype switching. The principal T cell response to extracellular bacteria is from CD4+ T cells in association with major histocompatibility complex (MHC) molecules.

Both antibodies and T cells perform several functions which serve to eliminate bacteria. IgG antibodies opsonize bacteria and enhance phagocytosis; IgM and IgG antibodies neutralize bacterial toxins and prevent their binding to target cells; and both IgM and IgG antibodies activate the complement system, leading to by-products that are mediators of acute inflammation.

Although the main purpose of our immune system is to protect us from foreign species, a large amount of cytokines or their uncontrolled production could be harmful. The most severe cytokine-induced consequence of infection by gram-negative bacteria is septic shock, where the principal mediators are TNF-α and IL-1.

A number of bacteria, many fungi, and all viruses survive and replicate within the host cells, acting as intracellular microbes. Among bacteria, the most pathogenic are those that are resistant to degradation by macrophages, and therefore survive within phagocytes. Resistance to phagocytosis is the reason why such bacteria tend to cause chronic infections that may last for years.

The major protective immune response to intracellular bacteria is cell-mediated immunity. It consists of two types of reactions: killing of phagocytized microbes by T cell-derived cytokines, particularly Interferon (IFN)-γ, and lysis of infected cells by CD8+ T cells. The protein antigens of intracellular bacteria stimulate both CD4+ and CD8+ T cells and lead to the differentiation of CD4+ T helper cells into Th1 cells caused by stimulated IFN-γ and IL-12 production.

Macrophage activation can also cause tissue injury. This may be manifested as delayed hypersensitivity reactions to microbial proteins and may also lead to chronic antigenic stimulation, such as in the histological hallmark, granulomatous inflammation. In this case, the host immune response is the principal cause of tissue injury and disease. Differences among individuals are important, though, as determinants of disease progression and clinical outcome.

Many viruses enter host cells by binding to physiological surface molecules. Three well-known viruses are human immunodeficiency virus-1 (HIV-1), which binds to CD4 molecules, Epstein-Barr virus (EBV), which binds to the complement receptor on B cells (CD21), and rhinovirus, the agent of the common cold, which binds to intracellular adhesion molecules (ICAM-1 or CD 54) which are expressed on a variety of cells, including the epithelium of the airway.

The intracellular persistence of viruses is their most obvious protective mechanism against effector cells and molecules, but viruses have also developed other forms of protection. Many viruses are capable of great antigenic variation and serologically distinct strains have been identified, such as those responsible for particular influenza pandemics. Some viruses suppress the immune system, resulting in an inhibition of the specific immune response. The most obvious is acquired immunodeficiency syndrome (AIDS) which is induced by HIV-1. One explanation is that pathogenic viruses may contain, or may have acquired, genes whose products inhibit antiviral immune responses.

Parasitic infection refers to infection with animal parasites, such as protozoa (parasitic worms), ticks, and mites. Such parasites currently account for greater morbidity and mortality than any other class of infectious organism. Humans are usually infected through bites from infected intermediate hosts. Protozoan and helminthic parasites that enter the blood stream or tissues are often well-adapted to resisting host defenses. Parasites elicit different immune responses to bacteria and viruses due to large variation in structure and biochemical properties. The major response to parasites is the production of specific IgE antibodies and eosinophils. The parasites stimulate the Th2 subset of CD4+ T cells, which secrete IL-4 and IL-5. Thus, IgE antibody binds to these opsonized organisms, eosinophils attach to them, secreting their granule content, and the major protein lyses the parasites.

Cells of the Immune System

The immune system comprises a variety of cells distributed throughout the body whose origin lies in stem cells found in the bone marrow. Various soluble substances are produced from the cells of the immune system and can be classified according to function.

In humans, the thymus is the central lymphoid organ and its main function is to stimulate the differentiation and proliferation of primitive bone marrow-derived lymphoid cells. The thymus is infiltrated with thymocytes, which are morphologically similar to blood lymphocytes.

The lymph nodes and the spleen are capsuled organs, through which foreign materials in the blood and lymph must pass and come into contact with macrophages and lymphocytes. They act as centers for phagocytosis and the initiation and development of the specific immune response. The three main types of specialized antigen-presented cells (APC)—macrophages, B cells, and DCs—are each specialized in processing and presenting antigens from different sources to naive T cells—those which have not yet acquired their antigen specificity. The activated T cells will then clonally expand and traverse the tissues as memory cells.

The cells mainly involved in the non-specific, innate, immune system are the phagocytic cells (monocytes, macrophages, NK cells, and neutrophils) and the mediator cells (basophils, eosinophils, mast cells, and platelets). The cells which are mostly involved in the specific immune system are the lymphocytes and plasma cells (Fig. 6.1).

Cells in the Innate Immune System

Monocytes and macrophages are members of the mononuclear phagocyte system, which after maturation can adopt a variety of morphologic shapes. When the cells first enter the peripheral blood after leaving the marrow they are incompletely differentiated. Once settled in the tissues, these cells mature and become macrophages. The cells are also sometimes called histocytes, and can be found in all organs and connective tissues. Many of their functions are critical for natural immunity, but they also play a central role in the specific acquired immune system. Macrophages phagocytize foreign particles such as microbes and macromolecules, including antigens, as well as body tissues which are injured or dead. They act as an APC since foreign antigens, after processing, are displayed on their surface in a form that can be recognized by antigen-specific T cells, activating production of IL-1.

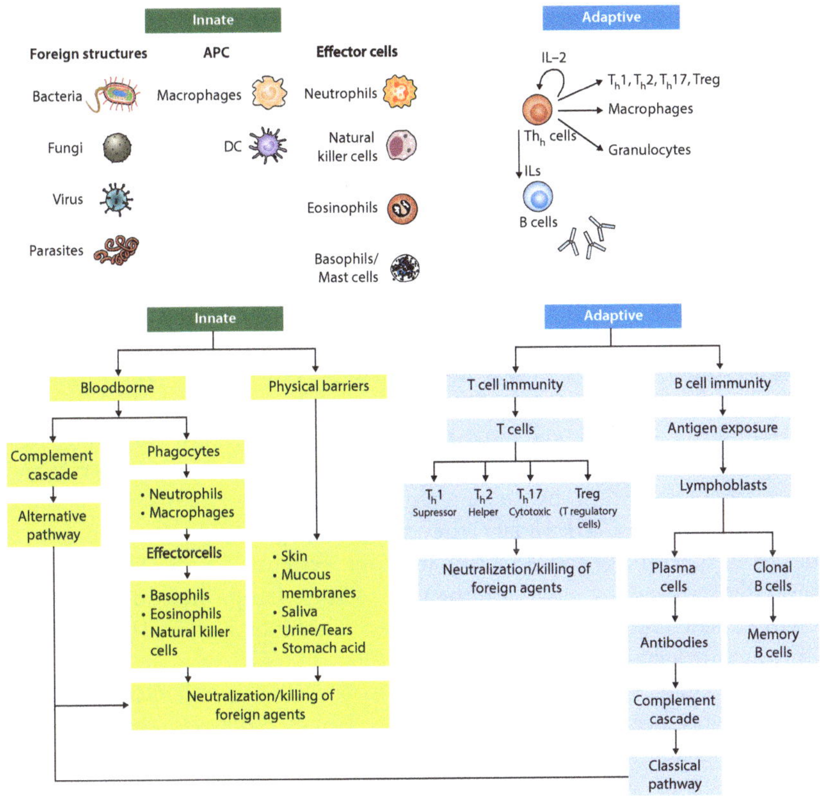

Fig. 6.1 Cells and substances in the innate and adaptive immune system. APC antigen-presenting cells, DC dendritic cells, IL interleukin, Th T helper cells, Treg T regulatory cells. (With permission from illustrator Jonny Hallberg, Sjöbo Sweden)

Macrophages play an important role both in inflammation and in immunity, and because of their potent activity, they may also cause tissue damage. When there is production of IL-1, IL-6, and TNF-α, they also act as a pyrogenic, as discussed below. Production of IL-10 results in Th2 activation, while production of IL-12 results in Th1 activation.

NK cells are large lymphocytes developed in the bone marrow from the same progenitor cells as T and B cells and contain numerous cytoplasmic granules which are capable of lysing a variety of tumor and virus-infected cells. NK cells are triggered by germ-line-encoded receptors that recognize molecules on the surface of infected or malignantly changed cells. They are found in blood and lymphoid tissues, and the spleen, but do not undergo thymic maturation. NK cells can be activated to increase their ability to lyse target cells by IFN-γ, IL-2, IL-12, and TNF. The production of IFN-γ by NK cells may influence the CD4+ T cell response to infectious agents, as they differentiate into pro-inflammatory Th1 cells able to activate macrophages.

The DCs leave the bone marrow in the form of immature lymphocytes, lacking dendrites, and expressing low levels of class II MHC and high levels of CD4. The DCs are known to be the main antigen-presented cells which migrate to most tissues in the body. They have a central functional role in driving immune responses since they are efficient at presenting protein antigens to T cells in lymphoid organs. The DCs are equipped with several mammalian Toll-like receptors (TLRs), which can detect the presence of infection by recognizing various components of bacteria, fungi, and viruses [10]. In fact, they are the key players in the interactions between the innate and adaptive immune systems. These TLRs induce several responses together with the two co-stimulatory molecules, namely, CD80 and CD86. They induce several chemokines such as IL-8 and the inflammatory cytokines IL-1β and IL-12.

Neutrophils, eosinophils, basophils, and mast cells are leukocytes called granulocytes because they contain abundant cytoplasmic granules, and they participate in the effector phase of specific immune response. They are referred to as inflammatory cells since they play important roles in inflammation and natural immunity and function to eliminate microbes and injured or dead tissue. Peripheral blood contains three types of granulocytes: neutrophils, eosinophils, and basophils. Neutrophils are the most numerous, respond rapidly to chemotactic stimuli or phagocytosis, and can be activated by cytokines. Eosinophils are particularly effective at destroying infectious agents that stimulate the production of IgE such as helminths. Their growth and differentiation are stimulated by T-cell-derived IL-5. Basophils act like mast cells but circulate in the blood. Both they and mast cells express high-affinity receptors for IgE. Interaction with these IgE molecules stimulates basophils and mast cells to secrete their granule contents, which are chemical mediators of immediate hypersensitivity (see Chap. 8) (Fig. 6.1).

Cells in the Adaptive Immune System

Precursor T cells arise in the bone marrow and then migrate to and mature in the thymus. T cells are subdivided into functionally distinct populations: the CD4+ T helper, or Th cells, and the CD8+ cytotoxic, or Tc cells. Their antigen receptors are membrane molecules and they recognize only peptide antigens attached to proteins that are encoded in the MHC. There are four subsets of Th cells: Th0, Th1, Th2, and Th17 effector cells or regulatory T cells (T regs). Naive T cells will differentiate upon antigen stimulation through an intermediate state termed Th0. The decision as to whether the Th0 will develop into an inflammatory Th1 cell, a helper Th2 cell, or a Th17 cell depends on interactions between environmental and genetic factors. The single most important factor is believed to be the cytokine environment at the site of priming.

The activities of the adaptive immune system are at nearly all times dependent on signals from a Th cell. Their signals also regulate the activities of the cells in the innate immune system. Th cells enact most of their helper functions by secreting cytokines. Typical cytokines secreted by human T cell subsets are: for Th1, IFN-γ and TNF-β; and for Th2, IL-4, IL-9, and IL-13. Cytokines produced by Th1 cells activate macrophages and the cytotoxic lymphocytes, resulting in a cell-mediated immune response. Cytokines produced by Th2 cells help to activate B cells, resulting in antibody production. Th17 cells, named because they produce IL-17, differentiate in response to IL-1, IL-6, and IL-23 [11]. The original function of Th17 cells is to protect the body against bacteria and fungi. Each subpopulation of Th cells can exert inhibitory influences on each other, and Th17 cytokines probably act as a bridge between the innate and adaptive immune responses. IFN-γ produced by Th1 cells inhibits the proliferation of Th2 cells and differentiation of Th17 cells, while IL-10 produced by Th2 cells inhibits production of IFN-γ by Th1 cells. IL-4 inhibits production of Th1 diurnal variation cells and differentiation of Th17 cells. Thus, the stimulation of the immune system is directed at the type of antigen that should be removed. Intracellular pathogens require a cell-mediated response, whereas antibodies are required for an extracellular response. Th17 cells are characterized by the production of a large amount of IL-17A, IL-17F, IL-21, and IL-22 [12]. IL-17 also enhances the severity of some autoimmune disorders (see Chap. 8).

A proper Th1/Th2 balance is important for ensuring effective repair of injury or elimination of an infectious organism, while at the same time minimizing damage locally. Too high a Th1 response can lead to cellular damage, while too high a Th2 response can lead to tissue damage [13]. It has been suggested that the Th1/Th2 balance may vary during the night and day due to diurnal variations in the levels of the immune modulatory hormones cortisol and melatonin [14]. Diurnal and seasonal changes in the immune system have been shown to correlate with melatonin synthesis and secretion [15]. Melatonin has also been found to decrease as aging progresses.

T regs are cells of the immune system which suppress the immune responses of other cells and act as a self-check [16]. The process of T reg selection is determined by the affinity of interaction with the self-peptide MHC complex. The immune system must be able to discriminate between the self and non-self. T regs exert their function by producing IL-10 and TGF-β, actively suppressing activation of the immune system, and preventing pathological self-reactivity [17] or autoimmune disease (see Chap. 8).

B cells acquired their name because in birds they were first shown to mature in an organ called the Bursa of Fabricius. In man, the early stages of B cell maturation occur in the bone marrow, where the specialized microenvironment provides signals that act on the lymphocytes to switch on key genes which direct the development program. The immature B cells carry an antigen receptor in the form of cell-surface IgM and can interact with their environment, resulting in the removal of self-reactive B cells. The next development step is for B cells to migrate to peripheral organs and mature, expressing both IgM and IgD on their surfaces. B cells with specific receptors for a particular antigen will trigger the production of a clone of B cells with identical specificity on exposure, and later, often develop into effector cells, which actively secrete antibodies, for example, plasma cells.

Plasma cells have a large nucleus, a plasma rich in ribonucleic acid, and an endoplasmic reticulum and ribosomes. These cells are very active in producing Igs. They are only found in lymphoid organs and at the sites of immune responses and normally do not circulate in the blood or lymph system. For example, effector cells generated in the mucosal immune system generally stay within the mucosal tissues. Plasma cells are believed to be terminally differentiated with little or no capacity for mitotic division.

Most of the lymphocytes generated by the clonal expansion of any given immune response event will die. A subset of the proliferating lymphocytes will persist and differentiate into memory cells, which can be much more quickly reactivated than naive lymphocytes if the same pathogen is encountered again. They are responsible for the long-lasting immunity that can follow exposure to disease or vaccination, which is called a memory response, or secondary immune response (Fig. 6.1).

A Toll protein was identified in the study of flies and found to be a crucial member of the innate system. The discovery of the family of Toll receptors in species as diverse as flies and humans, and the recognition of their role in distinguishing molecular patterns that are common to microorganisms, has led to a renewed appreciation of the innate system [18]. The mammalian Toll-like receptors (TLRs) are able to distinguish a very broad variety of different PAMPs, but the body must be able to respond differently to the various antigens. Today, 12 TLRs have been identified in humans, and most of them are widely expressed by different cell types in the immune system, including DCs, macrophages, NK cells, mast cells, neutrophils, B and T cells, as well as by non-immune cells such as fibroblasts, epithelial cells, and keratinocytes [19]. DCs patrolling peripheral tissues in the form of immature cells may be activated, including high expression of MHC and CD80 and CD86, and they then migrate to the lymph nodes to activate the antigen-specific naive T cells [20]. Which cell type is produced depends on the cytokine milieu surrounding the T0 cells. For example, IL-12 drives the transformation to Th1 cells and production of IFN-γ, whereas IL-4 leads to differentiation into Th2 cells producing IL-4, IL-5, IL-10, and IL-13. Uncontrolled regulation of TLR-mediated signaling may lead to excessive or persistent inflammation and severe immune pathology in the host [21]. Several diseases, including septic shock, autoimmunity, atherosclerosis, metabolic syndrome, and gastric cancer, have been linked to chronic or acute inflammatory response (see Chap. 8) (Fig. 6.2).

How does the immune system distinguish between food antigens and harmful antigens?

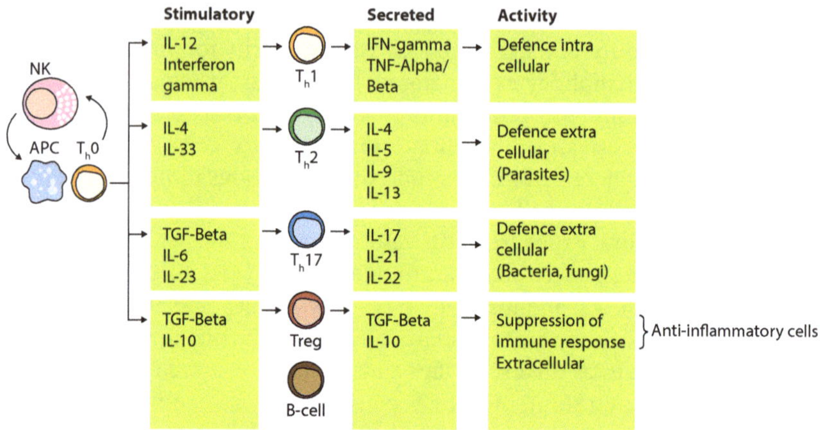

Fig. 6.2 Cells and their mainly secreted cytokines in the immune defense system. APC antigen-presenting cells, IFN interferon, IL interleukin, NK natural killer cells, TGF tumor growth factor, TNF tumor necrosis factor, Treg T regulatory cells, Th T helper cells. (With permission from illustrator Jonny Hallberg, Sjöbo Sweden)

Immunoglobulins

The protective effects of humoral immunity are mediated by a family of structurally related glycoproteins called antibodies or immunoglobulins (Ig), referring to the immunity-conferring portion of the gamma globulin fraction. Antigen-specific B cells bind to protein antigens via membrane Ig (B cell receptor) and internalize, process, and present MHC-associated peptide determinants to specific Th cells. This contact leads to B cell responses and the secretion of cytokines by the Th cells to stimulate the proliferation and differentiation of the B cell.

Th1 cells stimulate cell-mediated inflammatory reactions through activation of phagocytic cells (in particular, macrophages) and cytotoxicity. Th2 cells initiate the humoral immune system by activating naive B cells to produce IgM antibodies and induce Igs' class switch. Due to their differing functions, it has been suggested that Th1 and Th2 cells mediate defense against different infectious agents: Th1 acts more to combat intracellular microbes, whereas Th2 defends against extracellular infection.

Three Th cell-derived cytokines, IL-2, IL-4, and IL-5, contribute to B cell proliferation, and IL-4 and IL-5 are the most potent inducers of antibody secretion by the B cell. IL-6, which is produced by macrophages, T cells, and many other cell types, is a growth factor for already differentiated, antibody-secreting B cells. The interaction of a multivalent or bivalent antigen or anti-Ig antibody with membrane Ig on B cells results in cross-linking of Ig molecules and the transduction of a series of biochemical signals to the cell interior.

The nature of the antibody responses is influenced by the relative amounts of different cytokines produced at the site of lymphocyte stimulation. This is because various cytokines have selective effects on B cells, especially on heavy chain isotype switching, and because combinations of different cytokines may be synergistic or antagonistic. Furthermore, the T cell subsets produce different cytokines which have different effects on the B lymphocytes. Also, preferential activation of one or the other subsets by various antigens leads to qualitatively distinct humoral immune responses.

The basic Ig unit consists of two identical heavy chains and two light chains held together by disulfide bonds. The light chains are named kappa (κ) and lambda (λ), and the heavy chains, depending on various Ig classes or isotypes, γ, α, μ, δ, ε. The antibody-binding fragment (Fab) contains the amino acid sequence specific for the binding of the antigen, and the crystalline fragment (Fc) contains the amino acids giving the Ig class its specific functions. IgM (μ) is a large molecule consisting of five basic units (a pentamer), and is therefore restricted almost entirely to intravascular sites. IgM is the first antibody to be produced and is a result of the activation of previously unstimulated B cells because resting B cells express only IgM (and IgD, which is rarely secreted). This phase is called the primary antibody response. IgG (γ) is the most abundant form of Ig in the plasma, and because it consists of only one basic unit, it can diffuse into the interstitial fluid. Thus, it is found at both intravascular and extravascular sites. It plays a major role in the defense against foreign agents in both blood and tissues. IgG antibodies can activate the complement system, and thereby attract other cells to come to the site of action. IgG is produced later during the primary antibody response through isotype switching, but in larger amounts in the secondary antibody response thanks to memory cells from the first response. IgG can be further subdivided into four subclasses (IgG1, IgG2, IgG3, and IgG4).

IgA (α) is present in the serum and is the major Ig of the external secretory system found in saliva, tears, colostrum, and breast milk, as well as in nasal, bronchial, and intestinal secretions. In serum, IgA often exists as a single molecule; in secretions, it exists as two basic units (a dimer) attached to a secretory component. This substance is produced by cells in the mucous membrane, and protects the IgA in secretions from destruction by enzymes. IgA can be further subdivided into two subclasses (IgA1 and IgA2).

IgD (δ) is, together with membrane IgM, expressed on the surface of mature naive B cells, part of the B cell antigen receptor complex, and is also co-expressed on almost all mature B cells. However, the unique function of IgD is unclear. B cells expressing both IgM and IgD will not have undergone class switching.

IgE (ε) consists of one basic unit which is almost entirely bound to tissue mast cells and circulating basophils since they possess receptors for the Fc fragment of IgE. In helminthic infections and severe atopy, the concentration is increased as a result of stimulation of isotype switching. When an antigen binds to IgE which is pre-attached to the surface of these cells, there is a rapid release of a variety of mediators that collectively cause increased vascular permeability, vasodilation, bronchial and visceral smooth muscle contraction, and local inflammation. Antigens that elicit strong immediate hypersensitivity reactions are called allergens. IgE and eosinophil-mediated immune reactions are dependent on the activation of Th cells of the Th2 subset. These T cells secrete IL-4, which is required for isotype switching to IgE and promotes recruitment of eosinophils, and IL-5, which activates eosinophils.

Cytokines

One major way in which cells of the immune system communicate with each other and with other cells are through cytokines. As mentioned earlier, these can influence the growth, development, functional differentiation, and activation of lymphocytes and other leukocytes. Below, some cytokines are described in more detail according to their effects.

Pro-inflammatory Cytokines

Almost all cells can produce IFN-α and-β but mononuclear phagocytes are the major cell source for production of IFN-α, while for IFN-β it is the cultured fibroblasts. The most potent natural signal that elicits synthesis is viral infection. Its other functions are activation of the NK cells' lytic function and an increase in class I MHC molecular expression on virally infected cells. Both IFN-α and-β are pyrogenic and affect the set-point level in the hypothalamus [22], that is, they increase body temperature as a part of the acute-phase response. Both are also secreted during immune responses to antigens because antigen-activated T cells stimulate mononuclear phagocytes.

Tumor necrosis factor (TNF)-α is the principal mediator of the host response to gram-negative bacteria. The active components of gram-negative bacteria are lipopolysaccharides (LPS) derived from the bacterial cell wall. LPS is also called an endotoxin. The major cellular source of TNF-α is LPS-activated mononuclear phagocytes. TNF-α is a mediator of both innate and adaptive immunity and is an important link between specific responses and acute inflammation. TNF-α is also an endogenous pyrogen that acts on cells in the hypothalamic thermoregulatory regions of the brain to induce elevation of body temperature (see Chaps. 5 and 7). It shares this property with IL-1β. Both these cytokines are found in serum exposed to LPS. The increase in body temperature due to TNF-α or IL-1β is mediated by increased synthesis of prostaglandins by cytokine-stimulated hypothalamic cells. Inhibitors of prostaglandin synthesis, such as aspirin and paracetamol, block this action of TNF-α and IL-1. TNF-α acts on mononuclear phagocytes to stimulate the secretion of IL-1 and IL-6 and on hepatocytes to increase particular serum proteins. The spectrum of activities from proteins induced by TNF-α, IL-1, and IL-6 constitutes the acute-phase response.

The principal function of IL-1, similar to TNF, is as a mediator of the host inflammatory response in natural immunity. As with TNF-α, the major cell source is activated mononuclear phagocytes. Production is triggered by bacterial products such as LPS; by macrophage-derived cytokines such as TNF-α or IL-1 itself; and by contact with Th cells. Systemic IL-1 shares with TNF-α the ability to cause increased body temperature, to induce synthesis of acute-phase plasma proteins by the liver, and to initiate metabolic wasting. IL-1 has a natural, competitive inhibitor, IL-1 receptor antagonist (IL-1ra), which is structurally homologous to IL-1 and binds to IL-1 receptors, but which is biologically inactive.

IL-6 is produced by cells in the innate immune system such as DCs, monocytes, macrophages, mast cells, B cells, subsets of activated T cells, tumor cells, fibroblasts, endothelial cells, and keratinocytes. IL-6 causes the hepatocytes to synthesize a number of proteins, such as fibrinogen, which contribute to the acute-phase response. Depending on the cellular source of IL-6, cytokines such as IL-1, TNF-α, PDGF, IL-3, granulocyte-macrophage colony-stimulating factor (GM-CSF), and IL-17 are important inducers of IL-6 [23]. IL-6 also serves as a growth factor for activated B cells late in the sequence of B cell differentiation.

The IL-17 family consists of six isoforms, IL-17A-F, produced by Th17 cells. Both IL-17A and F (also known as IL-25) induce multiple pro-inflammatory mediators, including IL-6 and IL-8. The effect is the recruitment of myeloid cells, particularly neutrophils, to the site of infection. IL-17 also stimulates other cells to secrete chemokines, including IL-6 and GM-SCF. IL-17A has been associated with many inflammatory diseases, such as rheumatoid arthritis (RA), asthma, and systemic lupus erythematosus (SLE).

IL-23 is a key cytokine for the interactions between the innate and adaptive immune systems, and it has a central role in driving early responses to microbes. Th17 cells express the IL-23 receptor and share a related structure with IL-12 which has a receptor on Th1 cells. In the early stage of an infection, DCs in this state are induced to synthesize IL-6 along with IL-23. T cells are key players in the adaptive immune response. Naive T cells (Th0) can become activated and can either differentiate into Th1, Th2, or Th17 cells. IL-23 acts on Th17 cells and promotes their expansion, which contributes to the clearance of extracellular bacteria and fungi [24]. IL-23 seems to have a special role in intestine immunopathology'.

Cytokines as Regulators of Lymphocyte Activation, Growth, and Differentiation

IL-2 is the principal cytokine responsible for the progression of T lymphocytes' cell cycle and is produced by antigen-activated Th cells. It acts on the cell that produced it (making it an autocrine growth factor), as well as on other nearby T cells. IL-2 stimulates the growth of NK cells and enhances their cytolytic function. It also acts on B cells, both as a growth factor and as a stimulus for antibody synthesis.

IL-3 and GM-CSF are released by both Th1 and Th2 cells and stimulate the production of macrophages and granulocytes in the bone marrow. Both IL-3 and GM-CSF also stimulate the production of DC. GM-CSF and IL-4 also induce monocytes to differentiate into DC, whereas macrophage colony-stimulating factor (M-CSF) induces their differentiation into macrophages.

IL-21 is produced by activated Th2 cells and belongs to the IL-2 family. It acts as an autocrine factor to stimulate the development of Th17 cells [25]. IL-21 has an important role in the expansion of activated B cells and in class switching of Ig isotypes such as IgE [26].

Anti-Inflammatory Cytokines

IFN-γ is one of the longest known and best characterized cytokines. It was first described in 1965 [27] and is mainly produced by activated NK cells. It generally acts as an immune-enhancer, especially on cell-mediated responses. One of its major physiological roles is its ability to regulate MHC class I and class II expression on a variety of cell types. This increased expression is an important step during the inductive phase of an immune response. INF-γ also stimulates antigen-specific T and B cells' proliferation and differentiation and influences antibody class switching. It induces components of the complement cascade, as well as of the acute-phase response, for example, IFN-α and IFN-β are pyrogens and act so as to increase the set-point temperature (see Chap. 5).

IL-4 was initially called B cell growth factor-1 because of its role in the early stages of B cell activation. It is secreted by several types of cell, such as activated T cells, mast cells, basophils, and eosinophils. IL-4 has a unique and important role in regulating antibody production, hematopoiesis, inflammation, and the development of effector T cell responses [28]. IL-4 also induces the expression of MHC class II on B cells and reacts directly to antibody class switching in IgG4 and IgE. Thus, IL-4 plays a critical role in inflammatory reactions mediated by IgE and eosinophil. Later, IL-4 skews the conversion of T cells to Th2 cells. IL-4 inhibits the production of monocyte and macrophage-derived pro-inflammatory cytokines such as TNF-α, IL-1, IL-6, and prostaglandin (PG) E_2 [29, 30].

IL-5 is produced by the Th2 subset of helper T cells and by activated mast cells. The major action of IL-5 is to stimulate the growth and differentiation of eosinophils and to activate mature eosinophils to enable them to kill helminths. These activities are complementary to the activities of IL-4 and IL-10. IL-5 produced by Th2 cells activate eosinophils, which can have direct toxic effects on pathogens by releasing molecules such as major basic protein (MBP). The expansion and differentiation of IgA-switched B cells are driven by IL-5, as well as by IL-6, IL-10 and IL-21.

IL-10 is produced by the Th2 subset, as well as by some activated B cells, activated macrophages, and some Th1 cells. IL-10 was initially thought to be produced mainly by the Th2 subset, but now accepted also to other cells such as, activated macrophages, dendritic cells, some B cells. IL-10 usually displays suppressive effects on the immune system by inhibiting all surrounding auto-reactive T cells, regardless of autoantigen specificity. IL-10 has a polyclonal activation of B cells at least in SLE [31]. Along with IL-5, IL-6, and IL-21, IL-10 drives the differentiation of IgA-switched B cells.

IL-12, produced by macrophages and DCs, is an important regulator of cell-mediated immune responses because of its effects on NK cells and T cells. It stimulates IFN-γ production and enhances cytolytic activity and acts as a growth factor for NK cells. Like IFN-γ, IL-12 stimulates the differentiation of naive T cells into the Th1 subset. It also stimulates the differentiation of T cells into mature, functionally active CTLs. IL-12 is closely related in structure to IL-23. Th1 cells express a receptor for IL-12, whereas Th17 cells express the IL-23 receptor.

IL-13 is produced by Th2 cells, and similarly to IL-4 and IL-5, it stimulates eosinophils and mast cells and activates B cells. IL-13 increases intestinal permeability and induces enterocyte differentiation and apoptosis [32]. Increased epithelial cell turnover is a critical component of the response to parasitic worms. TGF-β, induced by IL-13, suppresses many inflammatory responses. These opposing immunological processes operate simultaneously in many parasitic infections and help to limit damage to the host. Similar to IL-4, IL-13 provides the first signal switching B cells to IgE production.

Macrophage migration inhibitory factor (MIF) has the unique property of being released from macrophages and T cells that have been stimulated by glucocorticoids. Once released, MIF overcomes the inhibitory effects of glucocorticoids on TNF-α, IL-1β, IL-6, and IL-8, and suppresses the protective effects of steroids against lethal endotoxemia. Glucocorticoids are considered to be an integral component of the stress response to infection or tissue invasion and serve to modulate inflammatory and immune responses. MIF counter-regulates the inhibitory effects of glucocorticoids and thus plays a critical role in the host control of inflammation and immunity [33].

Some cytokines have more distant effects. GM-CSF, like IL-3, is released by both Th1 and Th2 cells and stimulates the production of macrophages and granulocytes in the bone marrow. Both IL-3 and GM-CSF also stimulate the production of DCs. GM-CSF and IL-4 both induce monocytes to differentiate into DCs, whereas macrophage colony-stimulating factor (M-CSF) induces their differentiation into macrophages.

Cytokines with Both Pro-inflammation and Anti-inflammation Activity

TGF-β is a regulatory cytokine with pleotropic functions in T cell development, homeostasis, and tolerance. It is produced by multiple lineages of cells. TGF-β also promotes the growth of new blood vessels [34]. As a cytokine, it is potentially important because it antagonizes many lymphocyte responses. In this sense, TGF-β is an 'anti-cytokine' in that it is a signal for shutting off immune responses [35]. TGF-β is probably a switch factor for B cells into the IgA isotype and is thus important in mucosal immune responses.

IL-18 is a cytokine belonging to the IL-1 superfamily which is produced by macrophages and other cells. IL-18 works by binding to the IL-18 receptor, and together with IL-12, it induces cell-mediated immunity following infection with microbial products such as LPS. After stimulation with IL-18, NK cells and certain T cells release IFN-γ, which play an important role in activating the macrophages and other cells. In response to some intracellular infections, IL-18, assisted by IL-12, drives IFN-γ production by antigen-specific Th1 cells. In acute inflammation IL-18 has an important protective role, stimulating the production and repair of epithelial cells. IL-18, in combination with IL-12, has been shown to inhibit IL-4-dependent IgE and IgG1 production and to enhance IgG2 production in B cells. IL-18 binding protein (IL-18BP) can specifically interact with this cytokine, and thus, negatively regulate its biological activity.

Immunological Activity During Pregnancy

Pregnancy presents a significant challenge to the maternal immune system. The system has to accept a semiallogeneic fetus, a product of two histo-incompatible individuals. The role of inflammation is important and necessary for successful pregnancies. The maternal immune system is regulated by cytokines to protect the embryo and the fetus and to promote proper growth. During induction of tolerance to an allograft—the fetus—there is a decrease in Th1 cytokines such as IL-2 and IFN-γ and an increase in Th2 cytokines including IL-4 and IL-10. The first stage of pregnancy is a predominantly pro-inflammatory phase and the second phase is a predominantly anti-inflammatory phase, in which Th2 cytokines mainly function to suppress the pro-inflammatory environment. The last phase is parturition causing the contraction of the uterus, in which the pro-inflammatory milieu is predominant.

How is it possible that the fetus is protected from an immune attack from the mother?

The Complement System

The complement system is a complex enzymatic system composed of a series of serum and membrane proteins, which interact sequentially with one another to produce biologically active protein products. It was discovered in the 1890s as a complement to antibodies as it also coats the pathogen in a similar way to antibodies, so that the pathogen will more easily be destroyed by phagocytic cells. The system includes three pathways: the lectin pathway, initiated by soluble carbohydrate-binding proteins, that is, mannose, which binds to particular carbohydrate structures on microbial surfaces; the classical pathway, which is initiated by antigen–antibody complexes; and the alternative way, usually activated directly by the surfaces of the infectious organism. The pathways, using the complement (C) 3 protein, form enzymes which initiate the formation of a cytolytic protein complex. The biological functions of the complement system include cytolysis, opsonization of organisms and immune complexes for phagocytosis, triggering of the acute-phase response, enhancement of humoral immune responses, and solubilization and clearance of immune complexes. In general, the activation of components of the system involves enzymatic cleavage of each component into two fragments. One of the fragments joins the cascade and generates new enzymatic activity capable of cleaving the next component. Some of the other fragments, such as C3a and C5a, act as chemoattractants and recruit immune-system cells to the site of infection, causing inflammation. Regulation is achieved by the natural instability and short active life of some of the active components, as well as by specific inhibitors [36].

Acute-Phase Proteins

C-reactive protein, or CRP, was detected about 80 years ago during an investigation of patients with acute illnesses [37]. A non-antibody serum component was found to precipitate when reacting with an extract of *Streptococcus pneumonia*. The reaction was present during the acute phase of the disease and disappeared when the patients recovered. The reaction is against C-polysaccharide, which gave the protein its name. Activated CRP can rise within 24 to 72 hours from less than 1.0 mg/l to 500 mg/l with a half-life of 19 hours. This CRP reaction has been extensively used in clinics to evaluate the response to antibiotic therapy and to distinguish bacterial from viral infections [38]. CRP has been found to increase with age. One of the main physiological functions of CRP is an activation of the complement cascade. CRP-mediated activation appears to be essentially limited to the initial stage, C1 to C4 [39]. Minor CRP elevations have been shown to reflect a low-grade of vascular inflammation. Another way in which CRP regulates complement activation is by increasing the expression of complement-inhibitory proteins. Thus, CRP both participates in host defense and at the same modulates potentially harmful side-effects of the inflammation.

The serum amyloid A (SAA) family was originally considered to be comprised of only one circulating precursor of the amyloid from which its name is derived. The SAA family is now known to contain a number of differentially expressed apolipoproteins which are synthesized mainly in the liver. They are divided into two main classes based on their responsiveness to inflammatory stimuli, of which A-SAAs are the major acute-phase reactants. A-SAA is also potentially involved in the pathogenesis of several chronic inflammatory diseases.

Mannose-binding lectin (MBL) is present in low levels in the blood of healthy individuals, but is produced in increased amounts during the acute-phase reaction. By recognizing mannose residues on microbial surfaces, it acts as an opsonin and is recognized by monocytes, which express the macrophage mannose receptor and also activate the complement system.

Fibrinogen is synthesized in the liver and is essential for hemostasis, wound healing, fibrinolysis, and inflammation. Fibrinogen has diverse roles, several with widely differing functions, which results in a balance between hemostasis and thrombosis [40].

Haptoglobin is an acute-phase protein with a strong association with diseases which have inflammatory causes [41]. It acts on free hemoglobin released into the circulation. Its level in plasma increases several-folds if stimulated by infection, injury, or malignancy. TNF-α and IL-1 activate production of IL-6, which is the major inducer of haptoglobin. The protein is involved in modulating the immune response, in autoimmune disease, and in major inflammatory disorders because of its antioxidant and anti-inflammatory role. Haptoglobin has several roles both in the cellular and humoral activities of both the innate and adaptive systems. The protein is an established inhibitor of Th2 cytokine release and a week inhibitor of Th1 release [42]. α1-Antitrypsin (AAT) and α1-antichymotrypsin (ACT) are both synthesized in response to pro-inflammatory cytokines and protect against enzymes released by inflammatory cells, particularly those released from neutrophilic granules. ACT acts as a tumor marker and inhibits CTL-mediated lysis. α2-Macroglobulin (A2M) and its peptide binding function mediates cellular uptake by endocytosis. α1-Acid glycoprotein (AGP) or orosomucoid is controlled by a combination of the major regulatory mediators, glucocorticoids, and the cytokine network, as with IL-1β, TNF-α, and IL-6.

Pyrogenic Activity

Research on the pathogenesis of fever is today called 'cytokine biology' [43, 44]. At first, it was thought that bacterial products caused fever via the intermediate production of a host-derived, fever-producing molecule, or endogenous pyrogen. Bacterial products and other fever-producing substances were termed exogenous pyrogens. However, the discovery of the cytokine-like property of the TLR signal provided the explanation for why any microbial product can cause fever. Today it is more appropriate to assign the label pyrogenic cytokines to the particular class of cytokines which are intrinsically pyrogenic (Fig. 6.3) [45].

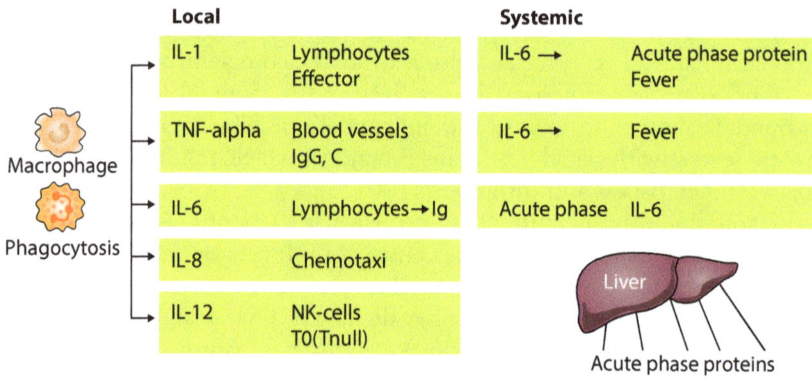

Fig. 6.3 Schematic view of the local and systemic response of the acute-phase reactions. C complement, Ig immunoglobulin, IL interleukin, NK natural killer cells, TNF tumor necrosis factor. (With permission from illustrator Jonny Hallberg, Sjöbo Sweden)

Pyrogenic activity can be produced by various pathogens, including viruses, yeasts, gram-negative and gram-positive bacteria, antigen-antibody complexes, and incompatible blood and blood products. The bacterial substance LPS, which is present in the cell wall of some bacteria, has a high grade of pyrogenic activity [46].

After birth, the sterile gut of the fetus rapidly becomes a reservoir for microorganisms [47]. Among infants in the neonatal intensive care unit a number of factors promote displacement of different microorganisms that are endemic to the local environment [48]. Protection by the mucosal barrier of the gut in premature and immune-incompetent infants offers imperfect protection against bacterial translocation [49]. Neonatal endotoxemia and release of pro-inflammatory cytokines, such as IL-1β, TNF-α, and IL-6, have been found to be important contributors to mortality in the neonatal intensive care unit [50].

PGs play a key role in the generation of inflammatory responses. They both sustain homeostatic functions and mediate pathogenic mechanisms, including the inflammatory response. Under physiological conditions, PGE_2 is an important mediator of many biological functions, such as regulation of immune responses, blood pressure, gastrointestinal integrity, and fertility. In inflammation, PGE_2 is of particular interest because it is involved in all processes leading to the classic signs of inflammation, that is, redness, swelling, and pain [51]. In addition, PGs of the E series are pyrogenic. Together with the understanding that non-steroidal anti-inflammatory drugs block fever by inhibiting PG synthesis, it is accepted that increased core temperature, or fever, is mediated by PGs, specifically PGE_2 [52]. The set-point temperature of the body will remain elevated until PGE_2 is no longer present or is suppressed by antipyretics, such as aspirin or paracetamol (see Chap. 5).

PGE_2 comes from the arachidonic acid pathway and is mediated by the enzymes phospholipase A2, cyclooxygenase-2 (COX-2), and prostaglandin E2 synthase. PGEs are found in most tissues and organs and are produced by almost all nucleated cells. PGE_2 can suppress Th1 differentiation, B cell functions, and allergic reactions [53]. Moreover, it can also exert anti-inflammatory actions on innate immune cells such as neutrophils, monocytes, and NK cells.

All pyrogenic cytokines are produced by phagocytic cells and cause an increase in the thermoregulatory set point in the hypothalamus. Major cytokines are IL-1 (α and β) and IL-6. Minor pyrogenic cytokines include CXCL8 (former IL-8), TNF-β, and IFN-α,-β,-γ [54].

Fever Phases

> Fever is a state of elevated core body temperature, which is often, but not necessarily, part of the defense of multicellular organisms (the host) against the invasion of live (microorganisms) or inanimate matter recognized as pathogenic or alien by the host. [55]

Since the regulation of body temperature is functioning normally when we have a fever, the course of temperature can be divided into three different phases: the chill phase, the plateau phase, and the defervescence phase (Fig. 6.4).

The chill phase begins when the immune cells react to foreign substances, causing a release of pyrogenic cytokines and, eventually, a rise in the set-point temperature to a higher level, which then is regarded as the desired body temperature (see Chaps. 5, 7 and 9; see Figs. 6.1 and 6.3). The neurons in the hypothalamus now receive information from receptors

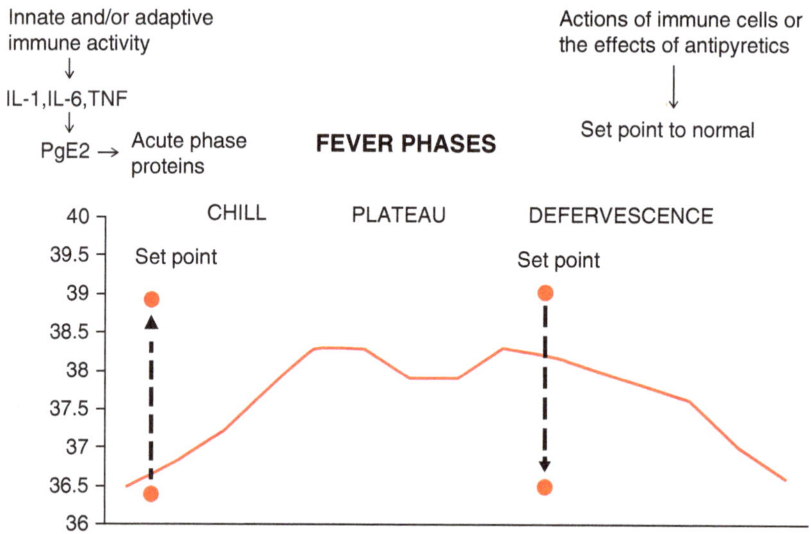

Fig. 6.4 Fever phases related to immune activity. IL interleukin, TNF tumor necrosis factor, PG prostaglandin. 40 °C (104 °F); 39.5 °C (103.1 °F); 39 °C (102.2 °F); 38.5 °C (101.3 °F); 38 °C (100.4 °F); 37.5 °C (99.5 °F); 37 °C (98.6 °F); 35.5 °C (97.7 °F); 36 °C (96.8 °F). (Copyright Grodzinsky, E and Sund Levander, M)

in the body about a temperature gradient and also perceive the circulating blood as cooler than the new, raised, set point. As a consequence the sympathetic nervous system is activated, stimulating muscle activity, which causes increased metabolism and vasoconstriction of skin vessels in order to preserve body heat. These reactions raise the body temperature until it equalizes to the new set point and the second phase, the plateau phase, begins. During this phase the body temperature is in balance with set point. When the set point returns to its normal level, because of the actions of immune cells or the effects of antipyretics, the third phase, the defervescence phase begins. During this phase the blood temperature is perceived as too hot compared to the set point of the neurons in the hypothalamus, and heat-releasing mechanisms, such as sweating, are stimulated [56].

Reflections

- How does the innate immune system identify pathogens?
- How do antibodies recognize antigens of a wide variety of different shapes?
- What are the major reasons that lymphocytes die without progressing beyond the pre-stage?
- What is the essential difference in function between B cells and T cells?
- Why do the functions of IgM and IgG class antibodies differ?
- Why are complement proteins present in the serum in unactivated form?
- How is the body alerted to an invasion by microbes?
- What are the roles of cytokine signals?
- Compare the immune response to extracellular versus intracellular bacterial pathogens.

References

1. Medzhitov R. Origin and physiological roles of inflammation. Nature. 2008;454:428–35.
2. Heinrich PC, Castell JV, Andus T. Interleukin-6 and the acute phase response. Biochem J. 1990;265(3):621–36.
3. Kato T, Kitagawa S. Regulation of neutrophil functions by proinflammatory cytokines. Int J Hematol. 2006;84:205–9.
4. Xing L, Remick D. Neutrophils as firemen, production of anti-inflammatory mediators by neutrophils in a mixed cell environment. Cell Immunol. 2004;231:126–32.

5. Janeway CJ, Medzhitov R. Innate Immune Recognition. Annu Rev Immunol. 2002;20:196–216.
6. Shi H, Deitch E, Da Xu Z, Lu Q, Hauser C. Hypertonic saline improves intestinal mucosa barrier function and lung injury after trauma-hemorrhagic shock. Shock. 2002;17:496–501.
7. Pillay J, Hietbrink F, Koenderman L, Leenen L. The systemic inflammatory response induced by trauma is reflected by multiple phenotypes of blood neutrophils. Injury. 2007;38(12):1365–72.
8. Hunt K, Walsh B, Voegel D, Roberts HC. Inflammation in aging part 1: physiology and immunological mechanisms. Biol Res Nurs. 2010;11(3):245–52.
9. Wikby A, Maxson P, Olsson J, Johansson B, Ferguson F. Changes in CD8 and CD4 lymphocyte subsets, T cell proliferation responses and nonsurvival in the very old: the Swedish longitudinal OCTO-immune study. Mech Aging Dev. 1998;102:187–98.
10. Bowie A. A46R and A52R from vaccinia virus are antagonists of host IL-1 and toll-like receptor signaling. Proc Natl Acad Sci. 2000;97:10162–7.
11. Infant-Duarte C. Microbial lipopeptides induce the production of IL-17 in TH cells. J Immunol. 2000;165:107–15.
12. Ghilardi N, Quyang W. Targeting the development and effector functions of Th17 cells. Semin Immunol. 2007;19:383–93.
13. Meneghin A, Hogaboam C. Infectious disease, the innate immune response, and fibrosis. J Clin Invest. 2007;117(3):530–8.
14. Gamble K, Berry R, Frank S, Young M. Circadian clock control of endocrine factors. Nat Rev Endocrinol. 2014;10(8):466–75.
15. Skwarlo-Sonta K. Melatonin in immunity: comparative aspects. Neuroendocrinol Lett. 2002;23:61–6.
16. Hori S. Control of regulatory T cell development by the transcription factor FOXp3. Science. 2003;299:1057–61.
17. Valencia, J, Watabe, H, Chi, A, Rouzaud, F, Chen K, Vieira, W, et al. Sorting of Pmel17 to melanosomes through the plasma membrane by AP1 and AP2: evidence for the polarized nature of melanocytes. J Cell Sci. 2006;119:1086–91.
18. Medzhitov R, Janeway CJ. The toll receptor family and microbial recognition. Trends Microbiol. 2000;8(10):452–6.
19. O'Neill L, Golenbock D, Bowie A. The history of toll-like receptors – redefining innate immunity. Nat Rev Immunol. 2013;13:453–6.
20. Touhg D. Type I interferon as a link between innate and adaptive immunity through dendritic cell stimulation. Leuk Lymphoma. 2004;45(2):257–64.
21. Beutler B. TLRs and innate immunity. Blood. 2009;113:1399–407.
22. Boehm L, Klamp T, Groot M, Howard J. Cellular responses to interferon-γ. Annu Rev Immunol. 1997;197:749–95.
23. Kishimoto T. Interleukin–6: from basic science to medicine—40 years in immunology. Annu Rev Immunol. 2005;23:1–21.

24. Korn T, Bettelli E, Oukka M, Kuchroo V. IL–17 and Th17 cells. Annu Rev Immunol. 2009;27:485–517.
25. Parrish-Novak J, Dillon S, Nelson A, Hammond A, Sprecher C, Gross J, et al. Interleukin 21 and its receptor are involved in NK cell expansion and regulation of lymphocyte function. Nature. 2000;408:57–63.
26. Leonard W, Spolski R. Interleukin–21: a modulator of lymphoid proliferation, apoptosis and differentiation. Nat Rev Immunol. 2005;5(9):68–98.
27. Wheelock E. Interferon-like virus-inhibitor induced in human leukocytes by phytohemagglutin. Science. 1965;149:310–1.
28. Brown M, Hural J. Functions of IL-4 and control of its expression. Crit Rev Immunol. 1997;17:1–32.
29. Corcoran M, Stetler-Stevenson W, Brown P, Wahl L. Interlukin-4 inhibition of prostaglandin E2 synthesis blocks interstitial collagenase and 92-kDa type IV collagenase/gelatinase production by human monocytes. J Biol Chem. 1992;267:515–9.
30. Lee J, Swisher S, Minehart E, Mc Bride W, Economou J. Interleukine-4 down-regulates interleukin-6 production in human peripheral blood mononuclear cells. J Leukocyt Biology. 1990;47:475–9.
31. Beebe A, Cua D, de Waal Malefyt R. The role of interleukin–10 in autoimmune disease: systemic lupus erythematosus (SLE) and multiple sclerosis (MS). Cytokine Growth Factor Rev. 2001;13(4):403–12.
32. Ceponis P, Botelho F, Richards C, McKay D. Interleukins 4 and 13 increase intestinal epithelial permeability by a phosphatidylinositol 3-kinase pathway. Lack of evidence for STAT 6 involvement. J Biol Chem. 2000;275(37):29132–7.
33. Calandra T, Bucala R. Macrophage migration inhibitory factor (MIF): a glucocorticoid counter-regulator within the immune system. Crit Rev Immunol. 1997;17(1):77–88.
34. Wahl S. Transforming growth factor-beta: innately bipolar. Curr Opin Immunol. 2007;19(1):55–62.
35. Gorelik L, Flavell R. Transforming growth factor-beta in T cell biology. Nat Rev Immunol. 2002;2(1):46–53.
36. Abbas A, Lichtman A, Pillai S. Cellular and molecular immunology. 6th ed. Philadelphia: Saunders; 2010.
37. Gotschlish E. C-reactive protein. A historical overview. Ann NY Acd Sci. 1989;557:9–18.
38. Du Clos T, Mold C. C-reactive protein: an activator of innate immunity and a modulator of adaptive immunity. Immunol Res. 2001;30:261–77.
39. Agrawal A. CRP after 2004. Mol Immunol. 2005;42:927–30.
40. Davalos D, Akassoglou K. Fibrinogen as a key regulator of inflammation in disease. Semin Immunopathol. 2012;34(1):43–62.
41. Quaye I. Haptoglobin, inflammation and disease. Trans Roy Soc Trop Med Hyg. 2008;102:735–42.

42. Arredouan M, Matthijs P, Van Hoeyveld E, Kasran A, Baumann H, Ceuppens J, et al. Haptoglobin directly affects T cells and suppresses T helper cell type 2 cytokine release. Immunology. 2003;108:144–51.
43. Atkins E. Pathogenesis of fever. Physiol Rev. 1960;40:580–646.
44. Beeson P. Temperature-elevating effect of a substance obtained from polymorphonuclear leucocytes. J Clin Invest. 1948;27(4):524.
45. Dinarello C. Infection, fever, and exogenous and endogenous pyrogens: some concepts have changed. J Endotoxin Res. 2004;10:210–22.
46. Bicego K, Barros R, Branco L. Physiology of temperature regulation: comparative aspects. Comp Biochem Physiol A Mol Integr Physiol. 2007;147(3):615–39.
47. Li M, Sanjabi S, Flavel R. Transforming growth factor-beta controls development, homeostasis, and tolerance of T cells by regulatory T cell-dependent and -independent mechanisms. Immunity. 2006;25(3):455–71.
48. Adams-Chapman I, Stoll B. Prevention of nosocomial infections in the neonatal intensive care unit. Curr Opin Pediatr. 2002;14(2):157–64.
49. Deitch E. Bacterial translocation or lymphatic drainage of toxic products from the gut: what is important in human beings. Surgery. 2002;131(13):241–4.
50. Sharma. Neonatal gut barrier and multiple organ failure: role of endotoxin and proinflammatory cytokines in sepsis and necrotizing enterocolitis. J Pediatr Surg. 2007;42:454–61.
51. Funk C. Prostaglandins and leukotrienes: advances in eicosanoid biology. Science. 2001;294:1871–5.
52. Ivanov A, Romanovsky A. Prostaglandin E2 as a mediator of fever: synthesis and catabolism. Front Biosci. 2004;9:1977–93.
53. Saper C, Romanovsky A, Scammel T. Neural circuitry engaged by prostaglandins during the sickness syndrome. Nat Neurosci. 2012;15:1088–95.
54. Walter F, Boulpaep E. Medical physiology: a cellular and molecular approach. Philadelphia: Saunders; 2003.
55. IUPS TC. Glossary of terms to thermal physiology. Pflugers Archives. 1987;410:567–87.
56. Sund Levander M. Body temperature (Kroppstemperatur) In: Edberg AW, H Wijk, editors. The base for nursing care health and illness (Omvårdnadens grunder Hälsa och ohälsa) in Swedish. 3 ed. Lund: Studentlitteratur; 2014.

General Reference

Murphy K. Janeway's immunobiology. New York: Garland Science; 2016.

CHAPTER 7

Assessment and Evaluation of Body Temperature

Evaluation of body temperature is an important sign of health and disease, in everyday life, for medical decisions, for nursing care, and when ordering laboratory tests. When assessing body temperature, we have to understand thermoregulatory mechanisms, and also consider several 'errors', such as the influence of gender, age and the site of measurement. When definitions of normal body temperature as 37 °C (98.6 °F) and 'fever' as 38 °C (100.4 °F) was established in the 1900 century, little was known about thermoregulation, immunology, and microbiology. Although today there is a general acceptance of body temperature as a range rather than a fixed temperature, the 1871 definitions of normal body temperature and fever still are considered the world-wide norm.

Normal Body Temperature

The definition of normal body temperature as 37 °C (98.6 °F) with 38.0 °C (100.4 °F) as fever was formulated in the middle of the nineteenth century by the German physician Wunderlich [1] at the time when thermometers were being introduced into medical practice (see Chap. 3). However, at that time there was little or no knowledge about the physiological mechanisms of body temperature regulation, the influence of hormones, cellular metabolism, physical activity, immunology, the inflammatory response, or microbiology. Neither were there suitable methods

E. Grodzinsky, M. Sund Levander (eds.), *Understanding Fever and Body Temperature*, https://doi.org/10.1007/978-3-030-21886-7_7

for calibration of thermometers. In addition, the measurements were performed on patients who were ill, indicating that a large number may have been febrile. Finally, axillary measurements were used, which gives only an estimate of peripheral temperature [2], and the measurements were performed in a non-standardized way. Since 1869 the development of the technical design of thermometers has been much improved, especially their technical accuracy [3]. This has been confirmed by Mackowiak et al. [4], who showed that the thermometer used at that time measured 1.4 °C (34.5 °F) to 2.2 °C (36 °F) higher than modern digital devices.

Although today there is a general acceptance of body temperature as a range rather than a fixed temperature, the 1871 definitions of normal body temperature and fever still are considered the world-wide norm. As consequence there is a widespread confusion of the assessment and evaluation of body temperature [5]. In addition, a systematic review showed there was a lack of studies performing body temperature measurements in a standardized way [6]. Galen and Gambino [7] further stated that a concept of normality is itself inadequate for the proper interpretation of test results if it is not interpreted in relation to a reference value. Hence, when assessing what is normal body temperature it is significant to consider variations *between* as well as *within* individuals.

Reflect on concept of normality in different contexts over time.

Differences Between Individuals

In most people, the circadian rhythm ensures that body temperature is at its lowest between three and four o'clock at night, with a circadian variation of approximately 19–20 hours (see Chap. 5) [8]. The diurnal rhythm is individual and constant both in health and disease. Recent research also shows that body temperature in healthy subjects varies some tenths of degree over time. Figure 7.1 shows the differences between the highest and lowest reading of five repeated measurements of oral, axillary and ear temperatures, performed at the same time with the same thermometers for five consecutive days. The figure also illuminates differences within individuals—the temperature gradients between different sites of measurement [9], as is discussed in more detail below (Fig. 7.1).

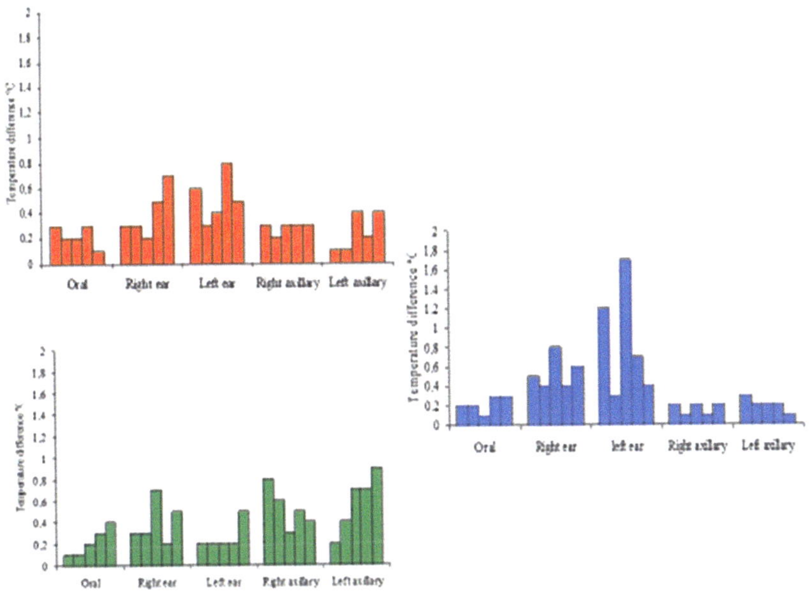

Fig. 7.1 Individual variability of five repeated measurements in the oral, right and left ear, and right and left axillary morning body temperature (C) performed in five consecutive days in three volunteers: (a) Subject 1, (b) Subject 2, and (c) Subject 3. Each bar represents the difference between the highest and the lowest value of five measurements in one morning. (Adapted from Sund Levander et al. [9]). (With permission from Wiley Publishing)

Gender

Women in general have a higher average body temperature compared to men [5, 10]. This is especially prominent in adolescents who have a higher body temperature compared with smaller children and adults, probably explained from hormonal influences in young girls [5]. Another example would be the increase in temperature after ovulation and during pregnancy [11]. This difference in body temperature seems to disappear after the menopause since body temperature in postmenopausal women does not differ from that of men of the same age, while both groups have lower temperatures compared with premenopausal women [9].

It is suggested that women maintain thermal equilibrium at higher ambient temperatures than men, and that they have a higher sweat onset and lower sweating capacity when exposed to heat [12]. Furthermore, women generally have a thicker layer of subcutaneous fat, which helps to insulate the core from heat gain during hot conditions.

Age

Children are traditionally expected to have a higher temperature than adults, because they are growing and moving more, and because body heat is produced as a by-product of increased metabolism. Though, recent research show that body temperature in children, aged 2 and 4 years, do not differ from adults and milled-aged individuals [5]. This study with 2006 individuals aged 2–89 years included, also reported that mean ear temperature was 36.4 °C ± 0.6 °C (97.5 °F ± 33.1 °F) overall and in the child and adult groups. In adolescents, it was 36.5 °C ± 0.5 °C (97.7 °F ± 33.0 °F), and in elderly > 65 years 36.1 °C ± 0.5 °C (97.0 °F ± 33.0 °F). In addition, about 25% had a normal ear body temperature below 36 °C (96.8 °F).

In older individuals, thermoregulation is thought to be primarily impaired due to age-related factors, such as a reduced proportion of heat-producing cells, a decrease in the total body water content, and in the metabolic rate and the sweating rate in response to body warming. There is also a delayed and reduced vasoconstriction and vasodilation response [13–17] as consequence to impairment and disease. The sedentary life-style of the elderly might also lower heat production. Hence, elderly individuals would be expected to have a lower baseline body temperature. As consequence, older people may become cold more easily, and are more sensitive to fluctuations in the ambient temperature. For example, an elderly person is more likely to become cold after a shower, when the skin is cooled, and they find it more difficult to lose heat by sweating in a hot environment. Finally, an increased frequency of hypothermia [18] and an altered shivering response have been reported [14].

Lu et al. [19] showed large variations in body temperature when measured at different non-invasive sites in older people. However, no differences in the average normal body temperature in healthy elderly women and men have been found [6, 20]. In frail elderly people, physical and cognitive decline, dependency on others during the activities of daily life, and a body mass index of less than or about 20 might be related to an increased risk of a lower body temperature, for example an ear morning temperature of 35 °C (95 °F) to 36 °C (96.8 °F) [21]. Also, daily medication with analgesics has been found to be associated with a higher temperature [22], reflecting the possibility that pain in aged individuals is related to chronic low-grade inflammation with increased circulating levels of pro-inflammatory proteins and consequent fever [23] (see Chaps. 6 and 8). A meta-analysis showed that the mean rectal body temperature in individuals with Alzheimer's disease was significantly increased by 0.1 °C (32.2 °F) as consequence of local inflammatory reactions in the brain, when compared to healthy elderly subjects. The clinical importance of this increase, though, might be of lesser significance [24]. Alzheimer's disease is also related to changes in diurnal rhythm, such as a more fragmented diurnal sleep profile, with frequent nocturnal awakening and daytime sleepiness [25]. Hence, it may be that responsibility for altering the base line body temperature lies not with old age per se, but instead with physical impairment and disease.

How do you define healthy ageing?

Differences Within Individuals: Temperature Gradients Within the Body

The temperature in the pulmonary artery (PA) is generally considered the gold standard of core temperature [21, 26], though Yeoh et al. [26], also include the esophagus, the rectal and the tympanic sites. In practice, non-invasive sites, such as the oral, the rectal, the bladder, the axillary, the esophageal or nasopharynx sites have been used to provide a surrogate for the core temperature [21, 26–28], and in recent years the ear [5]. In clinical practice, especially the rectal site has been considered as estimating the 'true' body temperature. Therefore, by tradition, oral and axillary readings taken with mercury thermometers, were adjusted to the rectal temperature by adding 0.3 °C (32.5 °F) and 0.5 °C (32.9 °F), respectively [29]. Modern electronic and digital thermometers can be set to either an adjusted mode (where the reading is adjusted to a reference site) or an unadjusted mode (where the actual measured temperature is reported). For example, ear readings might be adjusted to the rectal, the PA or the oral site. How these adjustments are calculated is not made public and varies considerably between manufacturers [30–32].

How evidence-based are these adjustment between sites? In the classical work of DuBois [33] the core of the body was defined as the thoracic and abdominal contents, some of the muscles, and the brain. Peripheral areas were defined as the skin and a small amount of subcutaneous tissue. He, and later Ring et al. [34], pointed out the misconception of a single body temperature, and emphasized that there is not one, but several core body temperatures depending on temperature gradients between internal organs within the body. The variation in gradients varies between as well as within individuals [9, 34, 35]. It is expected that simultaneously measured temperature varies, which is confirmed in a controlled study with thermometers in the unadjusted mode. When simultaneously measured rectal, oral, ear and axillary temperatures was compared in healthy adult subjects, the deviations were −0.7 °C (−33.3 °F) to +2.8 °C (+37.0 °F) for rectal—ear; −1.4 °C (−34.5 °F) to + 2.3 °C (+36.1 °F) for rectal—axillary; and −1.5 °C (−34.7 °F) to +2.3 °C (+36.1 °F) for rectal—oral temperatures [9]. This illustrates that it is not possible to interchange different temperatures, or to claim that there is a single range of core body temperatures. Hence, there is no evidence for adjusting one site to another, as no factor exists which allows accurate use of temperatures recorded at one site to estimate the temperature at another [31, 35, 36].

Though, there is lack of studies performing temperature measurements in a standardized way [6]. Several systematic reviews [21, 37–40] of studies comparing the rectal, bladder, oral, ear, temporal artery, nasopharynx, pulmonary artery and esophagus sites in different constellations confirm the large variation between sites. However, in these systematic reviews the mode of the thermometers, e. g if there are adjustments between sites or not are not reported, which may influence the reported differences.

In addition, various parts of the body react differently when body temperature is rising and falling [39], e.g there is a lag time for adjustment to the set point temperature. The more far from hypothalamus temperature is measured the longer lag time for adjustment to set point temperature. Also, body temperature varies over the body due to lag time for adjustment to the set point temperature in hypothalamus [9, 34–36, 41]. Hence, when measuring body temperature, the unadjusted mode should be used without adjusting to another site [9, 31, 42]. It is crucial to remember that a thermometer always measure its own temperature and nothing else and that temperatures outside the hypothalamus are themselves estimates of the core temperature with their own variability. Taken together, in plain language when you measure at one site and claim to estimate another site, the temperature is measured in the wrong place and in the wrong time. The rational for this is based on thermoregulation and differences between and within individuals. Therefore, it is surprising that published systematic reviews [21, 37–40], in total summarizing results from 71 clinical trials, nor clinical practice guidelines for measuring body temperature in the emergency department [43], consider differences between sites and if the thermometers are adjusted to another site or not.

What is a true body temperature reading?

Reflect on a true value of core body temperature measurement.

Measurement of Body Temperature

The purpose of measuring body temperature is to estimate the core body temperature. As mentioned above, this is the temperature in the thoracic and abdominal contents and in some of the muscles and the brain, and it is not the peripheral temperature, that of the skin and subcutaneous tissue [33]. As invasive core temperature measurement is only a choice in patients with a central intravenous-line, noninvasive/peripheral sites are used instead. It is important to emphasize that non-invasive methods display estimated core temperatures values (offsets) rather than actual ones [21].

Digital electronic thermometers for invasive measurement, and rectal, oral and axillary devices, have a sensor which produces electronic signals, reflecting the tissue temperature. The temperature is displayed as an unadjusted or adjusted value either in a steady-state mode after the sensor has reached equilibrium or using a predictive mode [42]. The Infrared radiation ear thermometer (IRET) measures infrared heat waves in the aural canal emitted from the tympanic membrane [44] (see Chap. 4).

Site of Measurement

An optimal site for measuring the core body temperature would be one which quantitatively and rapidly reflects changes in the arterial temperature and would be expected to be stable in relation to the temperature of the internal organs, irrespective of circulatory changes or heat dissipation affecting the periphery, and in relation to external factors such as environmental temperature and humidity [34, 45]. The method should also be based on required degree of accuracy and precision (see Chap. 4), patient comfort, costs, fastness of measurement, need for training and risk for complications [21]. In clinical practice the rectal, oral, axillary, ear (aural canal) or the temporal artery (forehead) sites are used to measure body temperature noninvasively. A prerequisite for achieving the best possible accuracy in measurements is to follow the manufacturer's instructions. No method meets the requirements of 100% accuracy, and they all have their strengths and weaknesses. Mostly a beep or a certain time frame, indicates that the heating process, according to the manufacturer, has been completed and that the temperature can be read. Table 7.1 summarizes the pros and cons of common non-invasive sites (Table 7.1) [47].

What is your measurement site of choice? Why?

The Rectal Site

The rectal site is an indication of the deep visceral temperature, modified by the temperature of the skin of the buttocks, the iliac artery and the iliac vein. The large tissue mass surrounding the rectal site provides for a stable reading that is shielded from ambient temperature. The rectal area has no thermal significance of its own and it is far from the central nervous system as well as from the crossroads of circulation at the heart. Therefore, it significantly lags behind changes at other core sites, especially during rapid temperature changes such as warming and cooling during surgery or exercise, and when temperature is increasing in fever. The temperature measured here may be either higher or lower than the core temperature [26, 36, 44]. For example, in simultaneous measurements, the rectal temperature did not change during a 20-minute exposure to either cold or warm conditions, while oral and tympanic temperature both changed [48]. A lag during general anesthesia for 20 minutes has been reported [49], as well as during re-warming from cardiac surgery of up to 1.5 hours [46]. In patients with head injuries, the rectal temperature underestimates brain temperature by as much as 2.1 °C (35.8 °F) [50] and in cold conditions the difference can be as high as 2.3 °C (36.1 °F) [51].

In the steady state, the rectal temperature is higher than at other places [36, 48, 52] due to the low blood flow and high isolation of the area, leading to a low heat loss [53]. Also, the heat-producing activity of micro-organisms in faeces influences the reading, and a hard stool might obstruct adequate placement of the thermometer. As the measured temperature increases by 0.8 °C (33.4 °F) with each 2.5 cm the device is inserted, a standardized depth of 4 cm in adults [44] and 2–3 cm in children [2] has

Table 7.1 Pros and cons of different sites for body temperature measurements

Measurement site	*Technical design*	*Pros*	*Cons*
Rectal	Contact thermometer Digital electronic device A sensor produces electronic signals, reflecting the tissue temperature Temperature displayed in unadjusted value in a steady-state mode or a predictive mode	Assumed to assess core temperature Easy to perform	The reading is higher than at other places during steady state Affected by hard stool and heat-producing activity of micro-organisms in faeces Affected by inflammation around the rectum The thermometer has to be inserted 4 cm in adults and 2–3 cm in a child, to give a correct reading Serious lag time for adjustment to set point temperature, especially during rapid changes, such as cooling of the skin, exercise, fever and hypothermia Risk of nosocomial infection Risk of rupture of intestinal mucosa Embarrassing for the patient Intrusive for the patient
Oral	Digital electronic device A sensor produces electronic signals, reflecting the tissue temperature Temperature displayed in unadjusted, adjusted value or a predictive mode	Assess core temperature Easy to perform	Placement affects the reading, e.g. there is a difference between the posterior pocket and the front area and also between the posterior pockets Affected by salivation, previous intake of hot or cold food and fluids, smoking, gum chewing, and breathing with open mouth Contraindicated in unconsciousness, confused patients Contraindicated when there is a risk of seizures Inappropriate in individuals with in-cooperative or disturbed behavior Inappropriate in young children

(*continued*)

Table 7.1 (continued)

Measurement site	*Technical design*	*Pros*	*Cons*
Axillary	Digital electronic device A sensor produces electronic signals, reflecting the tissue temperature Temperature displayed in unadjusted, adjusted or a predictive mode	Convenient for the patient Might be reliable when measuring body temperature in babies under the age of 3 month	Do not assess core temperature Strongly affected by ambient temperature, local blood flow, underarm sweat, appropriate placing of the probe or closure of the axillary cavity, and duration of the reading The reading is lower compared to other sites in steady site Serious lag time for adjustment to set point temperature, especially during rapid changes, such as cooling of the skin, exercise, fever and hypothermia Unreliable for assessing body temperature
Ear (aural canal)	Infrared radiation device Estimating the infrared heat waves from the tympanic membrane	Assess core temperature Close to Hypothalamus Hygienic Rapid measurement Convenient for the patient Painless for the patient Do not threaten the patient's integrity	Gives low readings if incorrectly placed Training in operator technique is needed before performance The reading may be influenced by otitis Incorrect placement of the probe due to a narrow cavity may affect accuracy
Temporal artery (forehead)	Infrared radiation device Estimating the infrared heat waves from the skin above the tympanic artery	Convenient for the patient Might be reliable when measuring body temperature in babies under the age of 3 month	Do not assess core temperature Unreliable for assessing body temperature Strongly affected by local blood flow, placement of the device, moisture in the skin, the amount of subcutaneous fat, physical activity and ambient temperature The reading is lower compared to other sites in steady site Serious lag time for adjustment to set point temperature, especially during rapid changes, such as cooling of the skin, exercise, fever, and hypothermia,

Adapted from Sund-Levander and Grodzinsky [46]. (With permission from British Journal of Nursing) been recommended. However, the rectal site is unhygienic and can pose a risk of injury to the intestinal mucosa, especially in infants and in rectal surgery. There can also be an increase in physical and psychological stress and in embarrassment, anxiety, and physical discomfort [44, 54].

The Oral Site

As a branch of the external carotid artery perfuse the area of the posterior sublingual pockets the oral temperature follows changes in the core temperature [44]. The sublingual temperature differs between the posterior pocket and the front area by approximately 0.8 °C (33.4 °F) in afebrile and 1.6 °C (34.9 °F) in febrile subjects [55], as well as between the posterior pockets [56]. Other influencing factors are salivation, previous intakes of hot or cold food and fluids, gum chewing, smoking and rapid breathing [44, 57]. Also, earlier studies suggested that vasomotor activity in the sublingual area affects the measured temperature, so a fall in oral temperature during the increase of body temperature in febrile individuals occur due to a reduced blood flow [58, 59].

The Axillary Site

Several factors affect the accuracy of axillary measurement, such as ambient temperature, local blood flow, underarm sweat, inappropriate placement of the probe or closure of the axillary cavity, and duration of the reading [60]. In addition, temperature differences between the right and left axilla of up to 1.4 °C (34.5 °F) in the steady state has been reported, as well as a large variation in repeated measurements [9]. As axillary measurements, even with careful positioning, only slowly register changes in core temperature, the readings can widely deviate from other sites [61], especially during increased body temperature, assessed as fever, due to vasomotor activity. Therefore, monitoring the skin temperature is an insensitive technique for estimating the core temperature [2]. Despite the above described uncertainty in this method, the axillary site is still popular for measuring body temperature, especially in critical care [62, 63].

The Ear Site

The IRET measurement is based on the facts that the tympanic membrane and hypothalamus share a blood supply from the internal and external carotid arteries, and that the area is relatively devoid of metabolic activity. As the probe of the IRET is placed about 1.5 cm away from the tympanic membrane, the reading is a mix of heat from the tympanic membrane and the aural canal. To compensate for the deviation, there is an offset system included in the instrument [5, 64]. The accuracy of IRET for the tympanic membrane temperature and repeatability and accuracy for changes in the core temperature during physical exercise and warming is reported to be good. The ambient temperature may alter the reading, although no affect was found during facial cooling or fanning [48, 65–67], and Twerenbold, Zehnder et al. [68] found highly reproducible readings irrespective of penetration depth, side of measurement and acclimatization to room temperature. The influence of cerumen is inconsistent, with some reporting no clinical influence [56, 68, 69], concluding that routine ear inspection prior to the measuring is not warranted [68]. Others observed a higher variability and an underestimation by an average of 0.3 °C (32.5 °F) [57, 70]. The occurrence of otitis media has been associated with values 0.1 °C (32.2 °F) higher, while others have reported no effect [69, 71]. A narrow ear cavity and different ear anatomy between individuals may affect repeatability and accuracy, because of the difficulty of placing the probe correctly [26, 72]. A difference in temperature between the left and right ear indicates the impact of operator performance on the temperature readings [73]. Due to observed differences between left and right ear and poor repeatability, some advocate duplicate or triplicate ear temperature measurements [10, 74, 75], but it has been shown that repeated measurements do not improve reproducibility, and that one measurement is sufficient when the ear, the oral or the axillary temperature is measured [9].

The Temporal Artery Site (Forehead)

The temporal artery thermometers scanner records skin temperature of the fore-head and temporal area and to capture the highest values. The core temperature is then estimated by proprietary algorithms which also compensate for ambient temperatures calculated by the manufacturer [21]. This site fluctuates considerably due to perspiration, make-up, lotions, oils, hair, local blood flow, placement of the device, moisture in the skin, the amount of subcutaneous fat, physical activity and ambient temperature [76–78]. In addition, vasopressive medication, skin thickness, bone and tissue between the temporal artery and the skin, temporal artery atherosclerotic disease, postoperative vasoconstriction, and circulation of catecholamine concentrations may affect accuracy in adults [79]. The accuracy of the method is especially questionable during rapid changes in body temperature. As the absolute temperature at the outer surface of the head over the temporal artery and the target arterial temperature are not the same, adjustments depending on reference temperatures are programmed into the devices [80]. These offsets are trade secrets. Because of the many factors influencing accuracy, and the built-in adjustments, monitoring the skin temperature is an insensitive technique for estimating the core temperature [21, 39].

In summary, from both a technical as well as a clinical point of view, the accuracy and precision of the reading of body temperature, and its repeatability, are significant in ensuring a correct assessment. Accuracy also implies measurement of the 'actual' body temperature and a correct placement of the thermometer [81]. It is important to base the assessment and evaluation of any particular technique on evidence-based knowledge, and not on tradition and personal belief (see Chaps. 4 and 9).

Reflections

- Describe a thermometer that is accurate, patient safe, and not unpleasant for the individual.
- Reflect on what may affect accuracy in a clinical situation.
- Reflect on individual gradients and measurement sites.
- Reflect on body temperature measurements in different contexts and cultures.
- Reflect on why the axillary site is so popular in intensive care units and the consequences of this.
- Reflect on body temperature measurement from an ethical and patient safety point of view.

References

1. Wunderlich CA, Seguin E. Medical thermometry and human temperature. New York: William Wood & Co; 1871. 280 p.
2. Mackowiak PA. Clinical thermometric measurements. In: Mackowiak PA, editor. Fever basic mechanisms and management, vol. 2. Philadelphia/New York: Lippincott Raven; 1997. p. 27–33.
3. Sund-Levander M, Grodzinsky E. Accuracy when assessing and evaluating body temperature in clinical practice: time for a change. Thermology International. 2012;22(Appendix 1 Number 3):25–32.
4. Mackowiak PA, Worden G. Carl Reinhold August Wunderlich and the evolution of clinical thermometry. Clin Infect Dis. 1994;18:458–67.

5. Sund Levander M, Grodzinsky E. Variation in normal ear temperature. Am J Med Sci. 2017;354(4):370–8.
6. Sund-Levander M, Forsberg C, Wahren LK. Normal oral, rectal, tympanic and axillary body temperature in adult men and women: a systematic literature review. Scand J Caring Sci. 2002;16(2):122–8.
7. Galen, R and Gambino S, Beyond Normality: The Predictive Value and Efficiency of Medical Diagnosis, 1975, New York: Columbia University College of Physicians and Surgeons, John Willey& Sons.
8. Aschoff J, Kleitman N, Halberg F, Klinker L, Simpson H, Bonlen J. Seasonal changes in the circadian variation of oral temperature during wakefulness. Experientia. 1975;11:1296–8.
9. Sund-Levander M, Grodzinsky E, Loyd D, Wahren LK. Error in body temperature assessment related to individual variation, measuring technique and equipment. Int J Nurs Pract. 2004;10:216–23.
10. Chamberlain JM, Terndrup TE, Alexander DT, Silverstone FA, Wolf-Klein G, O'Donell R, et al. Determination of normal ear temperature with an infrared emission detection thermometer. Ann Emerg Med. 1995;25:15–20.
11. Baker F, Mitchell D, Driver H. Oral contraceptives alter sleep and raise body temperature in young women. Eur J Phys. 2001;424:729–37.
12. Cabanac M. Thermiatrics and behaviour. In: Blatties CM, editor. Physiology and pathophysiology of temperature regulation. Singapore: World Scientific Publishing Co. Pte. Ltd; 1998. p. 108–25.
13. Elia M, Ritz P, Stubbs R. Total energy expenditure in the elderly. Eur J Clin Nutr. 2000;54(Suppl 3):S92–103.
14. Frank S, Raja S, Bulcao C, Goldstein D. Age-related thermoregulatory differences during core cooling in humans. Am J Physiol Regul Integr Comp Physiol. 2000;279:349–54.
15. Kenney W, Munce T. Invited review: aging and human temperature regulation. J Appl Physiol. 2003;95(6):2598–603.
16. Minson C, Holowatz L, Wong B. Decreased nitric oxide- and axon reflex-mediated cutaneous vasodilation with age during local heating. J Appl Physiol. 2002;93:1644–9.
17. Pierzga J, Frymoyer A, Kenney W. Delayed distribution of active vasodilation and altered vascular conductance in aged skin. J Appl Physiol. 2003;94:1045–53.
18. Morita S, Matsuyama T, Ehara N, Miyamae N, Okada Y, Jo T, et al. Prevalence and outcomes of accidental hypothermia among elderly patients in Japan: data from the J-Point registry. Geriatr Gerontol Int. 2018;18:1427–32.
19. Lu SS, Leasure A, Dai Y. A systematic review of body temperature variations in older people. J Clin Nurs. 2010;19(1–2):4–16.
20. McGann KP, Marion GS, Lawrence D, Spangler JG. The influence of gender and race of mean body temperature in a population of healthy older adults. Arch Family Medicine. 1993;2:1265–7.

21. Kiekkas P, Stefanopoulos N, Bakalis N, Kefaliakos A, Karanikolas M. Agreement of infrared temporal artery thermometry with other thermometry methods in adults: systematic review. J Clin Nurs. 2016;25:894–905.
22. Sund-Levander M, Wahren LK. The impact of ADL-status, dementia and body mass index on normal body temperature in elderly nursing home residents. Arch Gerontol Geriatr. 2002;35:161–9.
23. Bruunsgaard H, Pedersen M, Klarlund Pedersen BK. Aging and proinflammatory cytokines. Current Opinion in Haematology. 2001;8:131–6.
24. Klegeris A, Schulzer M, Harper D, McGeer P. Increase in core body temperature of Alzheimer's disease patients as a possible indicator of chronic neuroinflammation: a meta-analysis. Gerontology. 2007;53:7–11.
25. Most E, Scheltens P, Van Someren E. Increased skin temperature in Alzheimer's disease is associated with sleepiness. J Neural Transm. 2012;119:1185–94.
26. Yeoh W, Lee J, Lim H, Gan W, Tan K. Re-visiting the tympanic membrane vicinity as core body temperature measurement site. PLOSone. 2017;17:1–21.
27. Mercer J. Glossary of terms for thermal physiology, third edition. Jpn J Physiol. 2001;51:245–80.
28. Pursell E, While A, Coomber B. Tympanic thermometry- normal temperature and reliability. Paediatric Nursing. 2009;21(6):40–3.
29. Betta V, Cascetta F, Sepe D. An assessment of infrared tympanic thermometers for body temperature measurement. Physiol Meas. 1997;18:215–25.
30. Earp JK. Thermal gradients and shivering following open heart surgery. Dimens Crit Care Nurs. 1989;8(5):266–73.
31. Sund-Levander M, Grodzinsky E. Time for a change to assess and evaluate body temperature in clinical practice. Int J Nurs Pract. 2009;15:241–9.
32. Terndrup TE. An appraisal of temperature assessment by infrared emission detection tympanic thermometry. Ann Emerg Med. 1992;21(12):1483–92.
33. EF DB. The many different temperatures of the human body and its parts. Western Journal of Surgery. 1951;59:476–90.
34. EFJ R, McEvoy H, Jungs A, Ubers J, Nachin M. New standards for devices used for the measurement of human body temperature. J Med Eng Technol. 2010;34(4):249–53.
35. McCarthy P, Heusch A. The vagaries of ear temperature assessment. J Med Eng Technol. 2006;30(4):242–51.
36. Sund-Levander M, Tingtröm P. Fever or not fever – that's the question: a cohort study of simultaneously measured rectal and ear temperatures in febrile patients with suspected infection. Clinical Nursing Studies. 2018;6(2):48–54.
37. Chen ZM, Zhiang XB, Li Long M, Yu Pu M. Accuracy of infrared ear thermometry in children: a meta-analysis and systematic review. Clin Pediatr. 2014;53:1158–65.

38. Niven D, Gaudet J, Laupland K, Mrklas K, Roberts D, Stelfox H. Accuracy of peripheral thermometers for estimating temperature: a systematic review and meta-analysis. Ann Intern Med. 2015;163:768–77.
39. Geijer H, Udumyan R, Lohse G, Nilsagard Y. Temperature measurements with a temporal scanner: systematic review and meta-analysis. BMJ Open [Internet]. 2016; 6:e009509.
40. Chiappin E, Venturini E, Remaschi G, Principi N, Longhi R, Tovo P, et al. 2016 update of the Italian pediatric society guidelines for management of fever in children. J Pediatr. 2017;180:177–83.
41. Grodzinsky E, Sund Levander M, editors. Assessment of fever. Physiology, immunology, measurement in clinical practice. Malmö: Gleerups; 2015.
42. Smitz S, Giagoultsis T, Dewe W, Albert A. Comparison of rectal and infrared ear temperatures in older hospital inpatients. J Am Geriatr Soc. 2000;48:63–6.
43. Zaleski M, Cooper M, Killuian M, Farnholtz-Province J, Gates K, Kamiensky M, et al. Clinical practice guideline: non-invasive temperature measurement. What method of non-invasive body temperature measurement is the most accurate and precise for use in patients (newborn to adult) in the emergency department? Clinical Practice Guideline: non-invasive temperature measurement. Emergency Nurses Association (ENA). 2015.
44. Blatties C. Methods of temperature measurement. In: Blatties C, editor. Physiology and pathophysiology of temperature regulation. Singapore: World Scientific Publishing Co. Pte. Ltd; 1998. p. 273–9.
45. IUPS TC. Glossary of terms to thermal physiology. Pflugers Archives. 1987;410:567–87.
46. Rotello L, Crawford L, Terndrup T. Comparison of infrared ear thermometer derived and equilibrated rectal temperatures in estimating pulmonary artery temperatures. Crit Care Med. 1996;24(9):1501–6.
47. Sund-Levander M, Grodzinsky E. Assessment of body temperature measurement options. Br J Nurs. 2013;22(14):16–23.
48. Zehner WJ, Terndrup TE. The impact of moderate ambient temperature variance on the relationship between oral, rectal, and tympanic membrane temperatures. Clin Pediatr. 1991;4:61–4.
49. Benzinger M. Tympanic thermometry in anaesthesia and surgery. J Am Med Assoc. 1969;209:1207–11.
50. Rumana CS, Gopinath SP, Uzura M, Valadka AB, Robertson CS. Brain temperature exceeds systemic temperature in head-injured patients. Crit Care Med. 1998;26(3):562–7.
51. Togawa T. Body temperature measurement. Clinical Physiological Measurement. 1985;6(2):83–102.
52. Milewski A, Ferguson KL, Terndrup TE. Comparison of pulmonary artery, rectal and tympanic membrane temperatures in adult intensive care unit patients. Clin Pediatr. 1991;4(Suppl):13–6.

53. Petersen M, Hauge H. Can training improve the results with infrared tympanic thermometers? Acta Anaesthesiol Scand. 1997;41:1066–70.
54. Fallis W. Oral measurement of temperature in orally intubated critical care patients: state-of-the-science review. Am J Crit Care. 2000;9(5):334–43.
55. Erickson R. Oral temperature differences in relation to thermometer and technique. Nurs Res. 1980;29:157–64.
56. Modell J, Katholi C, Kumaramangalam S, Hudson E, Graham D. Unreliability of the infrared tympanic thermometer in clinical practice: a comparative study with oral mercury and oral electronic thermometers. South Med J. 1998;91(7):649–54.
57. Rabinowitz RP, Cookson SY, Wasserman SS, et al. Effects of anatomic site, oral stimulation, and body position on estimates of body temperature. Arch Intern Med. 1996;156:777–80.
58. Cranston WI, Gerbrandy J, Snell ES. Oral, rectal and oesophageal temperatures and some factors affecting them in man. J Physiol. 1954;126:347–58.
59. Gerbrandy J, Snell ES, Cranston WI. Oral, rectal and oesophageal temperatures in relation to central temperature control in man. Clin Sci. 1954;13:615–24.
60. Bland J, Altman D. Statistical methods for assessing agreement between two methods of clinical measurement. Lancet. 1986;327:307–10.
61. Robinson J, Charlton J, Seal R, Spady D, Joffres M. Oesophageal, rectal, axillary, tympanic and pulmonary artery temperatures during cardiac surgery. Can J Anaesth. 1998;45(4):317–23.
62. Lee H, Inui D, Suh G, Kim J, Kwon J, Park J, et al. Association of body temperature and antipyretic treatments with mortality of critically ill patients with and without sepsis: multi-centered prospective observational study. Crit Care. 2012;16(R33):1–13.
63. Thompson H, Kagan S. Clinical management of fever by nurses: doing what works. J Adv Nurs. 2010;67(2):359–70.
64. Lefrant J-Y, Muller L, Emmanuel de La Coussaye J, Benbabaali M, Lebris C, Zeitoun N, et al. Temperature measurement in intensive care patients: comparison of urinary bladder, oesophageal, rectal, axillary, and inguinal methods versus pulmonary artery core method. Intensive Care Med. 2003;29:414–8.
65. Jakobsson J, Nilsson A, Carlsson L. Core temperature measured in the auricular canal: comparison between four different tympanic thermometers. Acta Anaesthesiol Scand. 1992;36:819–24.
66. Matsukawa T, Ozaki M, Hanagata K, Iwashita H, Miyaji T, Kumazawa T. A comparison of four infrared tympanic thermometers with tympanic membrane temperatures measured by thermocouples. Can J Anaesth. 1996; 43(12):124–8.
67. Shibasaki M, Kondo N, Tominaga H, Aoki K, Hasegawa E, Idota Y, et al. Continuous measurement of tympanic temperature with a new infrared method using an optical fiber. J Appl Physiol. 1998;85(3):921–6.

68. Twerenbold R, Zehnder A, Breidthardt T, Reichlin T, Reiter M, Schaub N, et al. Limitations of infrared ear temperature measurement in clinical practice. Swiss Med Wkly [Internet]. 2010;20. https://doi.org/10.4414/smw.2010.13131.
69. Chamberlain JM, Grandmer J, Rubinoff JL, Klein BL, Waisman Y, Huey M. Comparison of a tympanic thermometer to rectal thermometer and oral thermometers in a pediatric emergency department. Clin Pediatr. 1991;4(Suppl):124–9.
70. Doezema D, Lunt M, Tandberg D. Cerumen occlusion lowers infrared tympanic membrane temperature measurement. Acad Emerg Med. 1993; 2(1):17–9.
71. Robb P, Shahab R. Infrared transtympanic temperature measurement and otitis media with effusion. International Journal of Otorhinolaryngology. 2001;59:195–200.
72. Duberg T, Lundholm C, Holmberg H. Örontermometer inte fullgott alternativ till rektaltermometer (Ear thermometer not satisfactory alternative to rektaltermometer). Läkartidningen In Swedish. 2007;104:1479–82.
73. Lee V, McKenzie N, Cathcart M. Ear and oral temperatures under usual practice conditions. Res Nurs Pract. 1999;1(1):8.
74. Stavem K, Saxholm H, Smith-Erichsen N. Accuracy of infrared ear thermometry in adult patients. Intensive Care Med. 1997;23:100–5.
75. Childs C, Harrison R, Hodkinson C. Tympanic membrane temperature as a measure of core temperature. Arch Dis Child. 1999;80:262–6.
76. Bridges E, Thomas K. Noninvasive measurement of body temperature in critically ill patients. Crit Care Nurse. 2009;29:94–7.
77. Edling L, Carlsson R, Magnusson A, Holmberg H. Temperaturmätning i panna eller axill inte tillförlitlig: Metoder och termometrar jämförda med rektalmätning som referens (temperature measurement in forehead or axilla not reliable: methods and thermometers compared with rectal temperature as reference). Läkartidningen In Swedish. 2888;46-90(107):2010.
78. Liu C, Chang R, Chang W. Limitations of forehead infrared body temperature detection for fever screening for severe acute respiratory syndrome. Infect Control Hosp Epidemiol. 2004;25(12):1109–11.
79. Suleman M, Doufas A, Akca O, Ducharme M, Sessler DI. Insufficiency in a new temporal-artery thermometer for adult and pediatric patients. Anesth Analg. 2002;95(1):67–71.
80. Pompei M. Temperature assessment via the temporal artery; validation of a new method. Arterial heat balance thermometry at an exposed skin site: accuracy, comfort and convenience for patient and clinician. 1999.
81. Crawford D, Hicks B, Thompdon M. Which thermometer? Factors influencing best choice for intermittent clinical temperature assessment. J Med Eng Technol. 2006;30(4):199–211.

CHAPTER 8

Physiological and Inflammatory Activity in Various Conditions

Hypersensitivity

The adaptive immune response is a critical component of the host's defence against infection and is essential for normal health (see Chap. 6). Adaptive immune responses are sometimes elicited by antigens not associated with infectious agents, which can cause a wide spectrum of disease states affecting any of the organs of the body. Hypersensitivity reactions are usually classified into four broad immunological mechanisms using the scheme of Coombs and Gell (Type I–IV). Today it is clear that there is overlap in the mechanisms involved in these immunological responses.

Type I are immediate allergic reactions by Immunoglobulin (Ig) E-antibodies and are one of the most powerful effector mechanisms of the immune system (see Chap. 6). This type of reaction is related to the majority of allergies, such as those to pollen, food, or dust, which are caused by the individual becoming sensitized to antigens, or, in this case, allergens, by the production of IgE antibodies. IgE antibodies are produced by plasma cells and have an affinity to mast cells and basophils, and are mainly localized in the tissues. Binding of antigens to IgE cross-links the receptors and causes the release of vasoactive substances, resulting in increased vascular permeability, vasodilation, bronchial smooth muscle contraction, and local inflammation. The immediate reaction starts within seconds of allergen exposure. These mediators are of three classes: biogenic amines such as histamine; lipid mediators such as prostaglandin D2, leukotrienes,

E. Grodzinsky, M. Sund Levander (eds.), *Understanding Fever and Body Temperature*, https://doi.org/10.1007/978-3-030-21886-7_8

and platelet activating factor; and cytokines such as tumour necrosis factor (TNF)-α, Interleukin (IL)-4, IL-5, and IL-13. These cytokines produced by T helper (Th) 2 cells both amplify the Th2 response and stimulate the class switching of B cells to IgE production. The tendency towards overproduction of IgE is influenced by both genetic and environmental factors. If the allergen is introduced directly into the blood, for example, by a bee or wasp sting, or in an allergic response to food allergens, the body becomes immediately activated, resulting in a widespread release of mediators, called anaphylaxis. The symptoms can range from mild urticaria to fatal shock-loss of blood pressure, airways constriction, and swelling of the epiglottis. The inflammatory skin rash known as eczema is common in the general population. Allergic eczema may have various underlying allergic mechanisms, not all of which predominately involve IgE. Although allergy is often considered solely as Th2 driven, both Th1 and Th2 cytokines can contribute to the immune response. Atopic eczema is the result of a chronic inflammation, and in both atopic and non-atopic allergic eczema Interferon (IFN)-γ and TNF-α produced by T cells contributes to the pathogenesis.

Asthma is a chronic inflammatory disease in the airways due to the infiltration of immune cells, hypersensitivity, bronchoconstriction, and airway obstruction [1]. One of the most common types of asthma is allergic asthma. After exposure to allergens, the antigen is phagocytized by mucosal dendritic cell (DC)s, which will present the antigen to naive Th cells in the lymph node. The T cells differentiate to Th2 cells and through secretion of IL–4, IL–5, and IL–13 drive class switching to production of IgE by the plasma cells [2]. Allergic asthma usually requires daily preventive treatment, and asthmatic attacks can be life threatening.

Hypersensitivity reactions involving IgG antibodies are classified as Type II and Type III responses. Type II reactions occur when circulation of antibodies is combined directly with recognition of an individual's host tissues as foreign. An example is when drugs bind to the cell surface, resulting in antibodies binding to the receptor and subsequent destruction of the cell. The lesions are due to the binding of specific antibodies and not to the deposition of immune complexes formed in the circulation.

Type III hypersensitivity reactions (immune-complex diseases) can arise when antibodies are produced as a result of antigen exposure and form immune complexes which persist in the circulation. The size, the amount, the affinity, and the isotype of the immune complexes produced are of importance, whether they will be rapidly eliminated from the body or not. Larger immune complexes fix complement and are quickly cleared from the circulation by macrophages, but these have difficulty in the disposal of small immune complexes. Smaller complexes are soluble, so they penetrate the blood vessels and tend to be deposited in the vessels' walls, leading to leucocyte activation and tissue injury. Medium-sized complexes, formed when there is a slight excess of antigen, are viewed as being highly pathogenic. Damage results from the action of cleaved complement anaphylatoxins complement (C)3a and C5a, which mediate the induction of granule release from mast cells and recruitment of inflammatory cells into the tissue [3]. One example of human immune complex diseases is systemic lupus erythematosus (SLE) (see Chap. 6).

A local type III reaction called the Arthus reaction can be triggered in the skin of sensitized individuals. The immune complexes bind to mast cells and other leucocytes, generating a local inflammatory response. Fluid and cells enter the site of inflammation and the complement system is activated, leading to the production of C5a. A systemic type III reaction, serum sickness, can result from the injection of large quantities of a poorly catabolized foreign antigen. An example would be treatment with antivenin—serum from horses immunized with snake venom—in the treatment of people suffering from the bites of poisonous snakes. The symptoms are chills, fever, rash, arthritis, and sometimes inflammation of the kidney. The symptoms occur seven to 10 days after the injection [4].

Type IV hypersensitivity or delayed-type hypersensitivity is mediated by T cells. The reaction can depend on proteins such as insect venom or tuberculin, or direct contact with antigens (haptens) such as metals, paints, cosmetics, or food antigens, as in gluten-sensitive enteropathy (coeliac disease). The response is caused by Th1 cells which recognize the processed antigen by an APC and release inflammatory cytokines such as IFN-γ and TNF-β. The reactions develop more slowly and will take around 24–72 hours. These specific T cells, mast cells and eosinophils, together with Th1 and Th2 cytokines, orchestrate chronic allergic inflammation, such as asthma [1].

What about environmental role in the development of autoimmunity?

Autoimmune Diseases

Autoimmune diseases are pathological processes directed against the host's own tissues and are either organ-specific or systemic reactions, frequently involving the skin and the musculoskeletal system, and include both monogenic and polygenic diseases [5]. The process is a chronic activation of the immune system in which the innate immune system activates the adaptive immune system, which then causes an inflammation [6]. Patients affected with autoimmune diseases have autoantibodies or autoreactive antigen-specific T cells driving the disease process. The autoimmune process evolves through two phases. In the initiation phase, self-nucleic acids released during the apoptotic process are recognized and internalized by DCs through T-cell receptors, and IFN-α is produced. IFN-α stimulates DCs maturation, autoantigen presentation, B and T cell recruitment, and autoantibody production [7]. In the second phase, DCs internalize immune complexes containing autoantibodies and nucleic acids and produce IFN-α, which stimulates DCs and T cells, leading to the self-perpetuation of antibody production and inflammation [8]. Some individuals are genetically predisposed to autoimmunity, and many autoimmune diseases are more common in females than in males.

Examples of polygenic autoimmune diseases are rheumatoid arthritis (RA), SLE, systemic sclerosis (SSc), polymyositis, dermatomyositis, Sjögren's syndrome, and undifferentiated and mixed connective tissue disease (UCTD and MCTD). Some genes have been identified as causing autoimmune polygenic diseases, mostly those involved in the regulation of immune system reactivity. Pathogenetic triggers for developing autoimmune diseases include infections, vaccinations, and medication.

Signs and symptoms in autoimmune diseases can form a broad spectrum, depending on organ involvement and disease severity. Some patients show cold episodes of increased body temperature and rashes, while some experience fever lasting from a few days to several weeks, combined with fatigue, flu-like symptoms, and weight loss. Active autoimmune diseases are accompanied with increased body temperature and are particularly associated with infections due to immunosuppressive treatment [9]. It has been suggested that increased body temperature may have an important role in modulating inflammatory diseases and that combating this increase may be counterproductive [10]. In some autoimmune diseases, an increase of the Erythrocyte sedimentation rate (ESR) and levels of C-reactive protein (CRP) could be seen, but in general, these biomarkers have a low diagnostic accuracy. A better way to find biomarkers for autoimmune diseases is to measure specific autoantibodies.

Autoinflammatory Diseases

Autoinflammatory diseases are syndromes, also called periodic fever syndromes, which form a group of rare, hereditary, recurrent, unprovoked inflammatory disorders which occur in the absence of infection [11]. These conditions represent a failure of the normal mechanism which limits inflammation, caused by mutations in the genes controlling the life, death, and activities of inflammatory cells. Their characteristics are similar to autoimmune diseases in that the pathological processes are directed against the host's own body, and they are systemic, frequently involving the skin and the musculoskeletal system. The process is a chronic activation of the immune system in which the manifestations are more often periodic than progressive. Symptoms include recurrent fevers, fatigue, diffuse pain in the muscles, loss of appetite, and poor sleep. Specific effectors are that the innate immune system directly causes the tissue damage, mediated predominately by cytokines, particularly IL–1β. This is in contrast to autoimmune diseases when the innate system activates or dysregulates the adaptive immune system. Increased levels of neutrophils and acute phase proteins are seen during the episodes. In autoinflammatory diseases, there is no association with the MHC class II haplotype [6].

What are the consequences of permanently elevated body temperature in autoimmune and autoinflammatory diseases?

Immunodeficiency

Immunodeficiencies occur when one or more components of the immune system are defective. Primary immunodeficiency may be caused by inherited mutations in any of a large number of genes. Secondary immunodeficiency is acquired as a consequence of other diseases or environmental factors. The deficiency is classified as innate or adaptive depending on which component of the immune system is defective (see Chap. 6). Adaptive immune defects include combined immunodeficiencies which comprise T and B cell immunity, or those limited to antibody deficiencies alone. Innate immune defects include deficiencies of the complement system, phagocytes, and TLR signalling.

Selective IgA deficiency is the most common primary immunodeficiency [12]. IgA is the most abundant Ig in the human body, as it plays a major role in the respiratory and gastrointestinal tracts. It, therefore, forms the most intimate interface between the environment and the host body. Normal levels of IgA are age dependent, but the international definition of IgA deficiency is a level below 0.07 g/l after the age of 4 years, in the absence of IgG and IgM deficiencies. The relationship between immunodeficiency and autoimmune diseases is well established. IgA deficiency has also been found to co-exist with autoimmune diseases, allergies, and malignancies [13]. The pathogenesis of IgA deficiency may represent a failure of switched memory B cells, leading to increased incidence of bacterial infections or autoimmune disease.

Secondary immunodeficiency is common in cases featuring malnutrition, or as an adverse consequence of medical treatment. This particularly affects cell-mediated immunity, and death is frequently caused by infection. Both measles and tuberculosis are significant infections in malnourished children. Secondary immunodeficiency states are also associated with tumours such as leukaemia and lymphomas. A major complication of the cytotoxic drugs used in treatment is immunosuppression and increased susceptibility to infection.

The most extreme case of immune suppression caused by a pathogen is acquired immune deficiency syndrome (AIDS), caused by infection with the human immunodeficiency virus (HIV). HIV infection leads to a gradual loss of immune competence, allowing infection with organisms which normally would not be pathogenic.

Malignancies

Malignant tumours grow in an uncontrolled manner, invading tissues, and often metastasizing to grow at sites distant from the original tissue. Tumours are derived from the host tissue, and the malignant processes involve the expression of molecules on the tumour cells which are recognized as foreign by the specific immune system. Tumour antigens can be classified into two main groups, those recognized by T-lymphocytes, and those identified by antibodies raised in other species after immunization with the tumour. The tumour antigens recognized by T cells are cell proteins processed and presented as small proteins (peptide-MHC complexes) to either CD4+ or CD8+ T-lymphocytes. DNA viruses are involved in the development of several different tumours. For example, Epstein-Barr virus (EBV) is associated with B cell lymphomas and Hodgkin's lymphoma. Human papilloma virus (HPV) is associated with human cervical carcinoma. B cell lymphomas occur frequently in T cell immunodeficient individuals, including patients with AIDS, and recipients of kidney or heart allografts who are receiving immunosuppressive drugs. IL-1 has many, varied, and multiple biological effects in the mediation of a number of inflammatory diseases, which is related to its role in some of the basic biological functions. The balance between IL-1 and its antagonist IL-Ra may play an important role in the normal physiology of various organs and tissues.

Metabolic and Endocrine Disorder

Chronic inflammation is observed in metabolic and endocrine disorders, such as obesity. This low-grade inflammation, involved in the pathogenesis of type 2 diabetes, hypertension, atherosclerosis, fatty liver, cancer metastasis, and asthma in obesity, is not linked to any infection. There is no increase in neutrophil granulocytes, and there is no increased body temperature and malaise. The systemic inflammation occurs with elevated pro-inflammatory cytokines in the circulation and is due to a rapid expansion of adipose tissue. Adipocytes and adipose tissue macrophages are the major cells responsible for the production of inflammatory cytokines. A major function of adipocytes is to store fat, but they also secrete many cytokines and hormones as part of their endocrine activity. At the molecular level, this inflammation activity inhibits the insulin signalling pathway, and this disorder contributes to whole body insulin resistance [14]. The mobilization of fatty acids from adipose tissue to other tissues is controlled by the nervous system, and hormones and cytokines. The major pyrogenic cytokines such as TNF-α, IL-1, and IL-6 activate adipocytes through lipolysis, in which free fatty acids are generated from triglycerides and released into the blood stream. The most abundant protein within the adipocyte is adiponectin, which has been shown to have a broad range of biological effects such as insulin-sensitizing and anti-atherogenic actions [15]. An increase in fatty acids contributes to the pathogenesis of fatty liver disease and atherosclerosis. Caloric restriction decreases the circulating levels of inflammatory cytokines and signalling activities in a variety of tissues [16].

Diabetes

There are mainly two types of diabetes, Type 1 and Type 2. Type 1 diabetes is an autoimmune disease driven by T cells which kill the insulin-producing β-cells. The pathogenesis is multifactorial with contributions from genetic, immunological, metabolic, and environmental factors. This loss of self-intolerance often begins as a result of a virus infection and leads to the release of self-antigens and the production of inflammatory cytokines such as TNF-α and IL-1β. DCs in the pancreas take up β-cell-derived antigens and signals are delivered to the T cells which will differentiate into Th1, Th2, or T reg cells, depending on the nature of the signals (see Chap. 6) [17]. Type 2 diabetes is caused mainly by obesity and inactivity, which leads to insulin resistance [18].

Atherosclerosis

Cardiovascular diseases are the most frequent cause of death in developed countries. Besides dyslipidemia, inflammation has a crucial role in the process, where increased levels of CRP and serum amyloid A proteins reflect important inflammatory components. Atherosclerosis is the dominant cause of cardiovascular disease, including myocardial infarction, heart failure, stroke, and claudication. The development of atherosclerotic lesions involves both innate and adaptive immune mechanisms [19]. Low-density lipoprotein modified by oxidation or enzymatic modification is present at an early stage. Activated endothelium with the expression of adhesion molecules appears to be an early event, allowing monocytes and T cells to attach the endothelium and penetrate into the intima. Individuals with autoimmune diseases such as RA and SLE have an increased risk of mortality from cardiovascular disease [20]. Several pro-inflammatory cytokines such as IL-6 contribute to the development of atherosclerosis [21], and IL-32 may also be implicated in the inflammatory cascade [22]. Raised levels of CRP have been implicated as a risk marker for atherosclerosis, although it is not clear if CRP has a causative role.

Inflammation and Pain

Cytokines in pain and inflammatory processes form a very complex system. Pro-inflammatory cytokines are induced after injury and may act on neurons to facilitate central sensitization and hyperalgesia, and contribute to the pain state. The interplay between the immune and nervous systems is thought to be critical for the development and maintenance of neuropathic pain. Neuropathic pain arises following lesion or dysfunction of the somatosensory nervous system and may result in alterations to cognitive and emotional brain functions. It accompanies a variety of conditions such as postsurgical, central nervous system injury, viral infections, tumours, and metabolic disorders such as diabetes mellitus. IL-1α and- β are pro-inflammatory cytokines which have an effect on a variety of cells and play a key role in pain, as well as in acute and chronic inflammatory and autoimmune disorders (see Chap. 6). IL-1β also has important functions such as regulation of feeding, sleep, and temperature [23]. Overproduction occurs in diseases such as RA, neuropathic pain, inflammatory bowel disease (IBD), osteoarthritis, vascular disease, multiple sclerosis, and Alzheimer's disease [4].

Gout is an autoinflammatory disorder, caused by hyperuricaemia, and is one of the most painful acute conditions known to man. Deposits of monosodium urate crystals stimulate the production of IL-1β, leading to gouty arthritis. These gout attacks present clinically as highly inflammatory arthritis with intense redness, warmth, and pain, surrounding an affected joint and are associated with systemic symptoms such as increased body temperature and elevated markers of inflammation [24].

Complex regional pain syndrome (CRPS) is a chronic and often disabling pain disorder, more often affecting women than men. The pathophysiology is unclear, but the neurogenic inflammation and activation of the immune system play an important role in the persistent pain state. A relation between pro-inflammatory cytokines and the disease duration and overall pain has been found in subgroups of patients [25].

Trauma, Neurodegenerative Disorders, and Postoperative Conditions Following Surgery

The skin plays a critical role in protecting the body against physical trauma, pathogens, allergens, chemicals, ultraviolet (UV) radiation, and excessive water and electrolyte loss. Its other functions include insulation, temperature regulation, and sensation. Inflammatory processes occur in most major neurodegenerative disorders, including both acute conditions such as traumatic brain injury and stroke, and chronic disorders such as Alzheimer's disease, epilepsy, and Parkinson's disease [26]. Increased pro-inflammatory cytokine levels are seen in the brain and cerebrospinal fluid of individuals affected by neurodegenerative disorders. These same cytokines are also involved in thermoregulation. The mechanisms of inflammation in the brain, the cytokine-driven brain and core temperature changes, and their relation to cognitive alterations, are all still unclear [27].

Both critical illness and postoperative status are associated with hyperglycaemia, without previous evidence of diabetes [28]. Glucose is the preferential substrate during the critically ill condition and serves as adequate provision of energy to tissues. However, increased glucose levels affect the exacerbation of inflammatory pathways, decreased complement activity, and modification in the innate immune system [29]. During stress hyperglycaemia, a complex interaction between hormones and cytokines leads to peripheral insulin resistance [30]. The avoidance of hypothermia and excessive blood loss, a prolonged preoperative fasting period, and prolonged immobilization synergize to reduce perioperative insulin resistance.

Inflammatory Conditions and Depression

Physiologically, the sickness response to infectious agents is considered to be a broad spectrum of symptoms such as increased body temperature, decreased appetite, fatigue, and malaise. Another behavioural syndrome with an inflammatory component is depression, which appears after pro-inflammatory cytokines have been produced [31]. It has been suggested that a low grade of systemic inflammation contributes to the development. Elevated CRP levels have been found to be associated with psychological distress and depression in the general population [32].

Immunotherapy and Anti-inflammatory Drugs

Evidence suggests that Th17 cells mediate both the innate and adaptive immune systems against a variety of pathogens at different mucosal sites [33]. Within the last 15 years, a number of new drugs have been approved to treat autoimmune diseases, mostly using therapeutic antibodies [34, 35]. Each IL-1 binds to the same cell surface receptor (IL-1RI), which is present on nearly all cells. Once bounds to its receptor, IL-1 triggers a cascade of inflammatory mediators, chemokines, and other cytokines. Its antagonist, IL-1Ra, prevents receptor binding. Anakinra, the recombinant form of IL-1Ra, was the first selective IL-1Ra to receive approval from the US Food and Drug Administration (FDA). Monotherapy blocking of IL-1 activity in autoinflammatory syndromes results in a rapid and sustained reduction in the severity of the diseases, including reversal of inflammation-mediated loss of sight, hearing, and organ function [36]. Anti-CD20 monoclonal antibody therapy is one of the most successful uses of therapeutic antibodies and may be employed against a variety of diseases, such as chronic lymphocytic leukaemia, follicular lymphoma, non-Hodgkin's lymphoma, and RA [37].

Anti-inflammatory refers to the property of a substance or treatment of reducing inflammation. Anti-inflammatory drugs make up about half of analgesics, remedying pain by reducing inflammation, in contrast to opioids, which affect the central nervous system. Non-steroidal anti-inflammatory drugs (NSAIDs) alleviate pain by counteracting the cyclooxygenase (COX) enzyme. On its own, the COX enzyme synthesizes prostaglandins, creating inflammation. In general, the NSAIDs prevent prostaglandins from being synthesized, and thereby reduce or eliminate the pain. Some common examples of NSAIDs are: aspirin, ibuprofen, and naproxen. The newer specific COX inhibitors are not classified together with traditional NSAIDs, even though they presumably share the same mode of action. On the other hand, there are analgesics that are commonly associated with anti-inflammatory drugs, but which have no anti-inflammatory effects. An example is a paracetamol, called acetaminophen in the United States. As opposed to NSAIDs, which reduce pain and inflammation by inhibiting COX enzymes, paracetamol has recently been shown to block the re-uptake of endocannabinoids, which only reduces pain, which probably explains why it has a minimal effect on inflammation. Some drugs and toxins react chemically with host body proteins and form derivates that the immune system recognizes as foreign. This immune response can lead to inflammation, complement activation, and destruction of tissue (see Chap. 6).

Reflections

- Why is there seldom any increase in body temperature during an allergic reaction?
- Briefly discuss both antibody-dependent and T-cell-dependent mechanisms which initiate autoimmunity.
- What are the different mechanisms for developing Type 1 and Type 2 diabetes?
- How might secondary immunodeficiency occur?
- Briefly discuss the occurrence of increased core body temperature in patients with Alzheimer's disease.

References

1. Agrawal D, Shao Z. Pathogenesis of allergic airway inflammation. Curr Allergy Asthma Rep. 2010;10:39–48.
2. Takhar P, Corrigan C, Smurthwaite L, O'Connor B, Durham S, Lee T, et al. Class switch recombination to IgE in the bronchial mucosa of atopic and nonatopic patients with asthma. J Allergy Clin Immunol. 2007;119:213–8.
3. Parham P. The immune system. 3rd ed. New York: Garland Science; 2009.
4. Dinarello C. Infection, fever, and exogenous and endogenous pyrogens: some concepts have changed. J Endotox Res. 2004;10:210–22.

5. Doria A, Zesäszn M, ååBettiio S, Gatto M, Bassi L, Nalotto L, et al. Autoinflammation and autoimmunity: bridging the divide. Autoimmun Rev. 2012;12:22–30.
6. Theofilopoulos A, Gonzales-Quintial R, Lawson B, Koh Y, Stern M, Kono D. Sensors of the innate immune system: their link to rheumatic diseases. Nat Rev Rheumatol. 2010;6:146–56.
7. Kawasaki T, Kawai T, Akira S. Recognition of nucleic acids by pattern-recognition receptors and its relevance in autoimmunity. Immunol Rev. 2011;243:61–73.
8. Leadbetter E, Rifkin I, Hohlbaum A, Beaudette B, Shlomchik M, Marshak-Rothstein A. Chromatin-IgG complexes activate B cells by dual engagement of IgM and toll-like receptors. Nature. 2002;416:603–7.
9. Jayne D. Current attitudes to the therapy of vasculitis. Kidney Blood Press Res. 2003;26:231–9.
10. Kettritz R, Choi M, Salanova B, Wellner M, Rolle FC. Fever-like temperatures affect neutrophil NF-kappaB signaling, apoptosis, and ANCA-antigen expression. J Am Soc Nephrol. 2006;12:1345.
11. Galeazzi M, Gasbarrini G, Ghirardello A, Grandemange S, Hoffman H, Manna R. Autoinflammatory syndromes. Clin Exp Rheumatol. 2006;24:579–85.
12. Yel L. Selective IgA deficiency. J Clin Immunol. 2010;30:10–6.
13. Etzioni A. Immune deficiency and autoimmunity. Autoimmun Rev. 2003;2:364–9.
14. Kahn S, Hull R, Utzschneider KM. Mechanisms linking obesity to insulin resistance and type 2 diabetes. Nature. 2006;444:840–6.
15. Wolf A, Wolf D, Rumpold H, Enrich B, Tilg H. Adiponectin induces the anti-inflammatory cytokines IL-10 and IL-1RA in human leukocytes. Biochem Biophys Res Commun. 2004;323:630–5.
16. Fontan L, Klein S, Holloszy J. Effects of long-term calorie restriction and endurance exercise on glucose tolerance, insulin action, and adipokine production. Age (Dordr). 2010;32:97–108.
17. Unane B. Antigen presentation events in autoimmune diabetes. Curr Opin Immunol. 2012;24:119–28.
18. Donath MY, Shoelson S. Type 2 diabetes as an inflammatory disease. Nat Rev Immunol. 2011;11:98–107.
19. Hansson G, Libby P, Schoenbeck U, Yan Z. Innate and adaptive immunity in the pathogenesis of artherosclerosis. Circ Res. 2002;91:281–91.
20. Hahn B, Groosman J, Chen W, McMahon M. The pathogenesis of artherosclerosis in autoimmune rheumatic diseases: roles of inflammation and dyslipidemia. J Autoimmun. 2007;28:69–75.
21. Libby P, Ridker P, Hansson G. Progress and challenges in translating the biology of artherosclerosis. Nature. 2011;473:317–25.
22. Heinhus B, Calin P, van Tits B, Kim S, Zeeuwen P, van den Berg W, et al. Towards the role of interleukin-32 in artherosclerosis. Cytokine. 2013;64:433–40.

23. Dinarello C. Historical insights into cytokines. Eur J Immunol. 2007;37(Supl 1):S34–45.
24. Dalbeth N, Haskard D. Mechanism of inflammation in gout. Rheumatology. 2005;44:1090–6.
25. Alexander G, Peterlin B, Perreault M, Grothusen J, Swcwartzman J. Changes in plasma cytokines and their soluble receptors in complex regional pain syndrome. J Pain. 2012;13:10–20.
26. Heneka M, Kummer M, Latz E. Innate immune activation in neurodegenerative disease. Nat Rev Immunol. 2014;14:463–77.
27. Schultzberg M, Lindberg C, Forslin Aronsson Å, Hjort E, Spulber S, Oprica M. Inflammation in the nervous system-physiological and pathophysiological aspects. Phys Behav. 2007;92:121–8.
28. Dungan K, Braithwaite S, Preiser J. Stress hyperglycaemia. Lancet. 2009;373:1798–807.
29. Amour J, Brzezinska A, Jager Z, Sullivan C, Weirauch D, Du J. Hyperglycemia adversely modulates endothelial nitric oxide synthase during anesthetic preconditioning through tetrahydrobiopterin- and heat shock protein 90-mediated mechanism. Anesthesiology. 2010;112:576–85.
30. Bagry H, Raghavendran S, Carli F. Metabolic syndrome and insulin resistance: preoperative considerations. Anesthesiology. 2010;108:506–23.
31. Raedler H, Heeger P. Complement regulation of T cell alloimmunity. Curr Opin Organ Transplant. 2011;16:54–60.
32. Wium-Andersen M, Örsted D, Nielsen S, Nordestgaard B. Elevated c-reactive proteins levels, psychological distress, and depression in 73,131 individuals. JAMA Psych. 2013;70:176–84.
33. Guglan L, Khader S. Th17 cytokines in mucosal immunity and inflammation. Curr Opin HIV AIDS. 2010;5:120–7.
34. Chames P, Van Regenmortel M, Weiss E, Baty D. Therapeutic antibodies: successes, limitations and hopes for the future. Br J Pharmacol. 2009;157:220–3.
35. Rosman NP. Febrile convulsions. In: Mackowiak PA, editor. Fever: basic management and treatment. 2nd ed. Philadelphia: Lippincott Raven; 1997. p. 267–77.
36. Dinarello C, Simon A, van der Meer J. Treating inflammation by blocking interleukin-1 in a broad spectrum of diseases. Nat Rev Drug Discov. 2012;11:633–52.
37. Limm S, Beers S, French R, Johnson P, Glennie M, Cragg M. Anti-CD20 monoclonal antibodies: historical and future perspectives. Haematologica. 2010;95:135–43.

General Reference

Murphy K. Janeway's immunobiology. New York: Garland Science; 2016.

CHAPTER 9

Clinical Implications

The Adaptive Value of Elevated Body Temperature

Thompson [1] describes the concept of fever as an adaptive, coordinated, and systematic response to an immune stimulus and as a self-limiting response in which thermoregulatory control remains intact and generally requires no treatment. Increased body temperature is recognized as a component part of the acute-phase response [2] and has evolved to provide adaptive advantages for the host (see Chap. 6) [3]. Increased body temperature in fever response is not limited to mammals and birds. Ectothermic animals, such as vertebrates, annelids (segmented worms), and arthropods, such as insects and spiders, also increase their core body temperature in response to injury or infection. The persistence of increased body temperature through evolution is amazing considering the metabolic cost; an increase in the core temperature of 1 °C (33.8 °F) above the baseline requires approximately a 12% increase in the basal metabolic rate. Theoretically, temperatures greater than 43 °C (109.4 °F) are harmful to the body because proteins in the body's cells may denature. However, body temperature in fever rarely exceeds 40 °C (104 °F) and almost never reaches 42 °C (107.6 °F) due to the physiological control mechanism and its endogenous temperature-lowering agents, which work to protect against very high body temperature (see Chap. 5) [4]. The risk that humans could be overheated when febrile is a view that is based more on traditional beliefs than scientific facts. A growing body of

E. Grodzinsky, M. Sund Levander (eds.), *Understanding Fever and Body Temperature*, https://doi.org/10.1007/978-3-030-21886-7_9

research in immunology and neurophysiology has led to the insight that fever is an adaptive response to defend the body from threats [5–7]. Animal and cell-cultured experimental studies demonstrate that increased body temperature in fever response in acute pulmonary injury or infection augments the development of human adult respiratory distress syndrome (ARDS), including neutrophil accumulation, and loss of endothelial and epithelial barrier functions [1]. Clinical data includes evidence for the beneficial value of increased temperature [7, 8] and the adverse effects of antipyretics on the outcome of infectious diseases such as gram-negative bacteremia, septicaemia, peritonitis, chickenpox, influenza, and community-acquired pneumonia. In adults with rhinovirus infections, antipyretics increase the viral shedding and nasal signs and symptoms, suppressing the antibody response and prolonging the course of the disease. A recent review [2] showed fever to be associated with improved survival in patients of invasive bacterial infection generally but also that survival decreased when temperature exceeded 39.4 °C (102.9 °F), suggesting that there is a upper limit to the optimal febrile range. However, the risk–benefit relationship of fever in the infected host is a controversial issue, and increased body temperature assessed as fever is still treated as the origin of the disease rather than as a symptom [1].

Perceptions of Fever

The traditional view that the presence of fever can be judged from a single cut-off value, which is equal for all individuals, irrespective of their gender, age, and so on is still the paradigm in clinical practice and guidelines for diagnosing infectious diseases and inflammatory processes [1, 9]. However, there is a major variation worldwide on how to define the level of temperature elevation warranting the diagnosis 'fever' [1]. For example, parents in Brazil defined the cut-off value for fever between 37.4 °C (99.3 °F) and 38.7 °C (101.7 °F) as measured, above all, in the armpit [10]. In published studies investigating sensitivity and specificity for different methods to detect fever, the definition of a temperature indicating fever is commonly defined as >38.0 °C, though ranging from 37 °C (98.6 °F) to 40 °C (104.0 °F) [11–16].

Others refer to clinical guidelines which divide fever into range of grades according to the underlying disease or disorder in the body [17]. According to those guidelines, low-grade fever, from 36 °C (96.8 °F) to

38 °C (100.4 °F), is caused by an inflammatory response resulting from a low-grade infection, from allergy or from trauma to bodily tissue, such as injury, surgery, or thrombosis. Moderate to high-grade fever is defined as 38 °C (100.4 °F) to 40 °C (104.0 °F) and is associated with a more intensive inflammatory response, such as those caused by a systemic infection, for example, pneumonia. The third level, hyperthermia, 40 °C (104.0 °F) or higher occurs as a result of hypothalamic damage, an overheated environment, or bacteremia. The problem with such divisions into different levels of fever and cut-off values is that it is based on the assumption that the range of normal body temperature is close to 37 °C (96.8 °F) and that a 'true' fever is a temperature over the cut-off value, commonly 38 °C (100.4 °F). A more logical approach is that what should be regarded as fever is closely related to what is considered normal body temperature. That is, as normal body temperature shows individual variations, it is reasonable that the same should hold true for the febrile range [9, 18, 19]. This means that an essential prerequisite for using fever in terms of elevated body temperature as a diagnostic value is to assess the reading in relationship to individual baseline temperatures [9]. From a recent study, including 1700 non-infected individuals aged 2–89 years, it appears that the difference between measured normal body temperature, in this study at the ear site in the unadjusted mode, and what the individual themselves indicated as increased body temperature in fever is about 1.1 °C (34 °F) to 1.5 °C (34.7 °F) depending on sex and age [20]. The result founded the concept DiffTemp™, that is, at least 1.0 °C (33.8 °F) increase from normal, combined with malaise, as an accurate definition of temperature in fever [20]. Secondly, what is considered as temperature in fever is also related to the site of measurement depending on temperature gradients within the body [21, 22] and the need of lag time for adjustment to the set-point temperature [22], especially when body temperature is rising and falling (see Chap. 7) [23]. Figure 9.1 illustrates simultaneous measurements of rectal and ear body temperatures in patients with suspected infection. Which site indicates 'true' fever? Actually, both sites indicate elevated temperature in fever, though changes in the ear temperature reacts faster to body temperature changes and antipyretics while rectal temperature changes are smaller and slower. Adjustments from one temperature site to another do not give correct information for diagnosis, and hence is a risk of diagnostic error affecting the medical clinical decision-making (Fig. 9.1) [19].

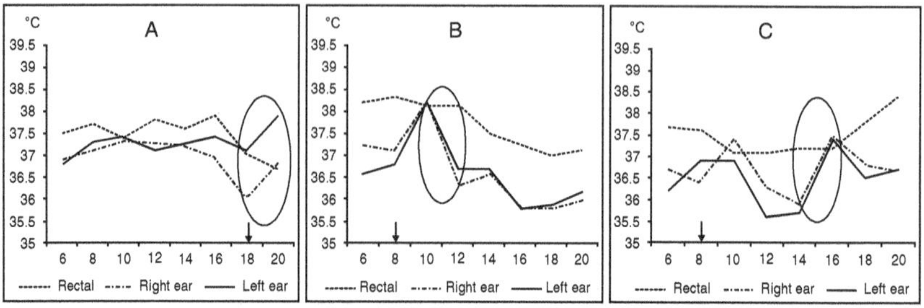

Fig. 9.1 Illustration of simultaneously measurements of rectal, right, and left ear body temperature in patients with infectious disease. Black arrows illustrate administration of paracetamol before measurement. Ovals illustrate the delay in change in rectal temperature A. Case 65. Woman, age 73, cared for pneumonia; B. Case 64. Man, age 64, cared for urosepsis; C. Case 13. Man, age 70, cared for pyelonephritis. 39.5 °C (103.1 °F); 39 °C (102.2 °F); 38.5 °C (101.3 °F); 38 °C (100.4 °F); 37.5 °C (99.5 °F); 37 °C (98.6 °F); 36.5 °C (97.7 °F); 36 °C (96.8 °F); 35.5 °C (95.9 °F); 35 °C (95 °F). (Adapted from Sund Levander and Tingström [19]. With permission from Clinical Nursing Studies)

Reflect on DiffTemp™ as an indication of temperature in fever. What substances do you think could be increased even if the body temperature does not exceed 38 °C (100.4 °F)?

Fever and Symptoms of Illness

> It ached in my head and I felt dizzy when I tried to get up. The fever beat with wet wings on my temples, and the aftershocks in my eye. I could no longer think clear thoughts. It glimmered and went black before my eyes, and I was unable to prevent humiliating tears wetting my pyjamas, I sank back on the damp pillow. … I must have raved loudly enough to be heard out in the hallway. The nurse came rushing, and I heard that they found me unconscious on the floor in front of the desk. [24]

The above quote is an experience of fever in tuberculosis in the early 1930s. The quote illustrates the typical symptoms of fear, anxiety, confused thinking, and powerlessness often associated with fever. Throughout history, cures for fever, therefore, aimed to 'expel evil', by bloodletting, vomiting, enemas, cooling of the skin, and sweat cures (see Chap. 2). In this way, it was believed the body would be purified and balance restored. These feelings of sickness, named malaise, are described as:

> a generalized feeling of discomfort, illness, or lack of well-being that can be associated with a diseased state. It can be accompanied by a sensation of exhaustion or inadequate energy to accomplish normal activities. [25]

In everyday usage, malaise tends to mean feeling vaguely unwell, lacking the energy to get up and do anything, or even just being lazy. However, there are few studies on individual perceptions of malaise which report individuals' descriptions of their symptoms when feeling ill. Ames et al. [26] asked patients with a cancer diagnosis who had a temperature above 38 °C (100.4 °F) about their experience of 'fever symptoms'. The patients reported weakness; feeling cold; warmth; sweating; non-specific bodily sensations, such as feeling awful or terrible; gastrointestinal symptoms, such as nausea; headache; emotional changes, such as feeling anxious, irritable, frustrated, or a general feeling of heightened emotions; achiness; and odd dreams and hallucinations. Respiratory symptoms such as cough, shortness of breath, and breathing difficulties were also mentioned as symptoms related to fever. Symptoms and signs related to increased temperature in fever described by nurses include observing that the patient experiences warmth, tachycardia, sweating, and changes in mental status, respiratory rate, and blood pressure [27]. In general, we are able to describe these feelings with words by ourselves, irrespective of age. However, critically ill patients, individuals with cognitive decline or disabilities, and small children might have difficulties in verbally expressing their sense of malaise. In these cases, observation of changes in signs and symptoms from normal behavior is a way to understand the individual condition. When signs and symptoms are non-specific, unclear, and/or blurred by comorbidities, increases in body temperature assessed as fever become crucial for the assessment of changed condition, for example, suspected infection.

What is malaise for you? What is your normal temperature? Should antipyretics be used when you have feelings of malaise?

Antipyresis

In order to lower body temperature, it is still common in nursing care to cool the skin when the patient is feverish [3, 28, 29]. Antipyresis refers to the symptomatic treatment of increased body temperature assessed as fever itself rather than of the underlying disease. The concept includes antipyretic therapy, such as pharmaceutical antipyretics, and physical methods to cool the body. The theoretical justification for antipyresis would be to reduce metabolic demands, for example, increased heart rate, decreased arterial blood pressure, and arterial oxygen.

Antipyretics

An antipyretic stimulus is defined as 'a stimulus or drug that can cause a decrease in body temperature of a febrile subject while having no effect on the body temperature of a normothermic or afebrile subject' [30]. Antipyretics could be justified if the metabolic costs of increased temperature assessed as fever exceed its physiological benefits, if the symptomatic relief exceeds the risk of affecting the course of the illness, and if the adverse effects of the drug are acceptable. Antipyretics have also been suggested in order to reduce mental dysfunction in frail elderly individuals with fever. In experimental studies with young volunteers, it has been shown that treatment with aspirin reduces mental impairment, although no study has confirmed this suggestion in elderly individuals [7, 31]. In patients with increased body temperature due to hyperthermia, external cooling is widely used and clearly indicated as these increases in body temperature are unresponsive to antipyretic drugs [32, 33], while the enhanced effects of antipyretics for elevated body temperature in febrile patients are yet to be understood by well-designed randomized controlled studies [8, 34]. Another reason for antipyretic therapy is to enhance patient comfort, which is supported as these drugs also have analgesic effects.

However, the costs of symptomatic relief in terms of drug toxicity and the course of the underlying illness have not been fully determined. If antipyretics are prescribed to patients, they should be administrated at regular intervals to prevent abrupt recurrences and not for temperature above some predetermined value [7].

Physical Antipyresis

The idea of cooling the body still persists in clinical care [35], despite a lack of reflection on the physiological basis for such interventions [9, 27]. Physical methods to lower body temperature assessed as fever include sponging with tepid water or alcohol using a circulating fan, with or without sponging [33, 36], ice packs, water cooling blankets [37], opening windows, and undressing the patient. In clinical practice, external cooling is initiated when body temperature exceeds a predetermined level [32]. The rationale for antipyresis in patients with increased body temperature assessed as fever differs in the literature. Nevertheless, the scope for lowering body temperature in fever with external cooling is limited, as it induces cutaneous vasoconstriction, vasospasm, shivering, sympathetic activation, rebound hypothermia, and discomfort [38, 39]. Of significant importance is the adverse effects in patients with underlying cardiovascular disease, as external cooling causes vasospasm of diseased coronary arteries by induction of a cold pressor response [39]. Hence, it is recommended to warm, rather than cool, selected skin areas in order to promote heat loss, thereby reducing vasoconstriction and preventing shivering [32]. Also, external cooling is opposed to normal thermoregulation mechanisms, resulting in increased heat production, metabolic rate, and oxygen consumption. Hence, cooling of the patient should always be preceded by antipyretics in order to lower the elevated thermostatic set point [39]. On the other hand, systematic reviews of published studies show that external cooling methods, comprising external cooling alone or combined with antipyretics, do not reduce increased body temperature assessed as fever in adults in acute care settings [33]. Others conclude that data reveal the limited effect of external cooling in critically ill patients due to metabolic and cardiovascular consequences [2].

A common reason for antipyresis is to enhance patient comfort. Nevertheless, it is still not clear exactly what symptoms are being treated and if antipyresis has any effect on patient comfort. Although it would seem reasonable to treat elevated body temperature in critically ill patients, clinical studies have not yet proved that antipyresis using antipyretics or external cooling has positive effects for patient outcome or comfort [26, 31]. It seems surprising that external cooling is still recommended in national guidelines and hospital 'fever management' protocols [37]. The administration of antipyretic drugs should be used selectively on an individualized basis, but they should always be given before physical cooling to prevent shivering [34]. In view of the adverse effects of external cooling it is questionable whether physical cooling methods should ever be used in feverish patients, especially severely ill patients, such as those in the intensive care unit (ICU) [7]. Interventions should instead focus on supporting the body's normal physiological processes, preventing complications, and promoting comfort based on the patient's wishes and the stage of the increased temperature in fever [17]. In short, if patients complain of cold, provide them with extra clothes or a blanket, and when they complain of too much warmth, remove the extra clothes or bedding.

Shivering

Shivering is the physiological emergency response to a rapid rise in body temperature [40] triggered by an increase in the gradient between the core and the peripheral (skin) temperature [41]. Shivering is very costly for the body in terms of increased sympathetic tone, oxygen consumption, respiratory minute volume, and a six-fold increase in metabolic rate [2]. Shivering is also unpleasant and painful for the patient and related to fatigue, exhaustion, and feelings of helplessness [42]. It can cause the core temperature to drift to the direction of the skin temperature. Thus, in febrile patients, antipyretics are necessary before the start of surface cooling so as to decrease the temperature gradient between the core and the periphery. Since the set point is already lowered by antipyretics, routine cooling of the skin could be seen as questionable [3]. Figure 9.2 illustrates a case when cooling of the skin in order to low body temperature in a severe cerebral injury patient triggers shivering [43]. At the beginning of the observation the gradient between the central (ear) and peripheral (toe) temperature is about 6 °C (42.8 °F) which increases to 17 °C (62.6 °F) (Fig. 9.2).

This example underlines the importance of knowing the physiology of thermoregulation and the consequences of antipyresis. According to thermoregulation, an increased temperature gradient between the core and the periphery triggers shivering. In this case, the gradient between the central and peripheral temperature is increasing because the set point is rising as a result of the acute-phase response. Because of the increased temperature gradient, the patient starts to shiver in order to equalize the central and peripheral temperatures [41]. The shivering causes the nursing staff, as a matter of routine, to measure the axillary temperature, which is an unreliable technique for estimating the core temperature [9, 44]. As the temperature is greater than 38.0 °C (100.4 °F) the nurse, following routine, begins cooling the skin with a fan and alcoholic wraps in order to lower the core body temperature. As a consequence of the thermoregulatory shivering response, though, the skin temperature has increased and, hence, decreased the temperature gradient to only 2 °C (35.6 °F). As this physiological response is not considered by the nurse, the cooling of the skin by the fan increases the temperature gradient once again, which

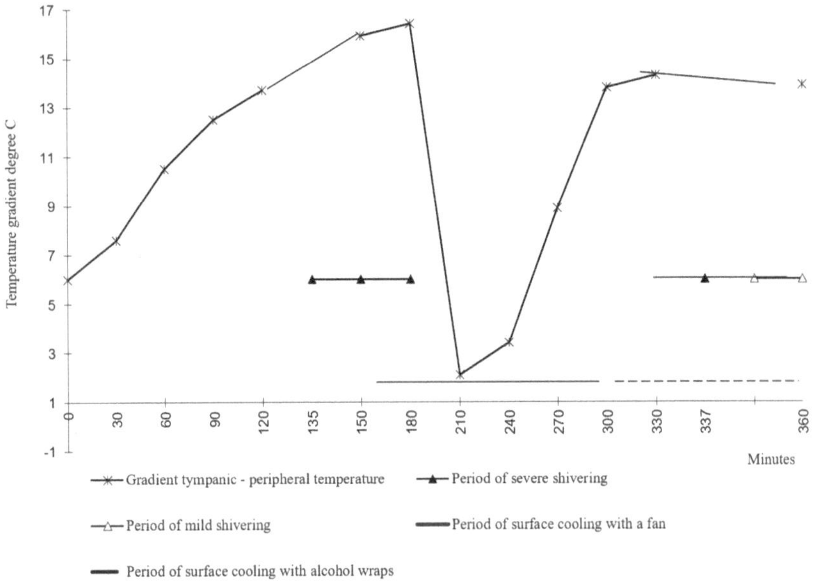

Fig. 9.2 An example for how surface cooling with alcohol wraps and a fan trigger shivering in a severe head injury Shivering is triggered by the increased temperature gradient in °C/°F: 17 °C (62.6 °F); 15 °C (59 °F); 13 °C (55.4 °F); 11 °C (51.8 °F); 9 °C (48.2 °F); 7 °C (44.6 °F); 5 °C (41 °F); 3 °C (37.4 °F); 1 °C (33.8 °F). (Adapted from Sund Levander and Wahren [43]. With permission from Wiley Publishing)

triggers further shivering. This example emphasizes the importance of giving the patient antipyretics before surface cooling starts [45]. One way to prevent shivering, when the patient is cooled or the ambient temperature is low, is to apply the knowledge of arteriovenous shunts and cold sensitive receptors located at the forearms, hands, lower legs, feet, and head (see Chap. 5). By covering those parts with quilted fabrics or towels, the gradient between the set point and the peripheral temperature is not increased and shivering is therefore not triggered [43, 46]. With the knowledge we have about thermoregulation and the risk of shivering when cooling febrile patients, it should be obvious that these procedures should be abandoned in clinical care.

Fever in the Critically Ill

Approximately 35% of in-hospital patients will develop fever, increasing to 70% in the critically ill in the ICU. Elevated body temperature may cause serious metabolic cost, especially the risk of increased intracranial pressure, and worsen secondary ischemic damage in patients with neurologic illness [47]. Therefore, control of temperature in patients with traumatic brain injury, intracerebral hemorrhage, acute ischemic stroke, and so on is a common recommendation within international guidelines [48], and physical cooling methods for lowering temperature are still routinely used in ICU settings worldwide [11].

However, the balance of benefit to harm from increased temperature in fever is complex in critically ill patients in the ICU [8]. In a large multicenter study, it was found that non-steroidal anti-inflammatory drugs (NSAID) or paracetamol independently increased 28-day mortality for patients with sepsis but not for non-septic patients [49]. A review of randomized controlled studies found no differences in mortality in feverish ICU patients treated with antipyretic agents or placebo [50]. Launely et al. [8] emphasize that the decision to start antipyretic therapy in an ICU patient should be based on the presence of cerebral injury or underlying cardiac disease and the absence of sepsis, while others report that changes in heart rate, arterial blood pressure, arterial oxygen saturation, and respiratory rate are either non-existent or too small to be of clinical significance [51, 52]. This means that for the majority of patients in an ICU, the metabolic burden of temperatures below 40 °C (104 °F) can be well tolerated without leading to hemodynamic or respiratory instability [52]. Also, improved outcome from antipyretics on neurological outcome in acute ischemic stroke is not completely clear [48]. A meta-analysis of randomized trials found no evidence that fever treatment influenced mortality in critically ill patients without brain injury [53]. It has been suggested that antipyretics should modulate the adverse effects of pyrogenic cytokines in patients with bacterial sepsis. However, studies show that although the temperature, heart rate, oxygen consumption, and levels of lactic acid were lowered, neither the incidence of organ failure nor 30-day mortality was decreased [32]. In patients with severe sepsis hypothermia, that is, below 36.5 °C (97.7 °F), was associated with increased mortality and organ failure, irrespective of the presence of septic shock [6]. Niven and Laupland [48] give prominence to the lack of clinical data for an evidence-based approach to fever control with antipyretic therapy. Until further data are available, they recommend antipyretic therapy to any patient with acute neurological injury, patients with temperature over 40 °C (104 °F), compromised cardiovascular physiology and elevated temperature, refractory shock, lactic acidosis, or multisystem organ failure. They do not recommend control of body temperature in patients with infection. Doyle et al. [54] suggest that the question should not be 'should we treat pyrexia', but 'in what conditions is it not beneficial to treat pyrexia'? They summarize from a narrative review that pyrexia treatment is beneficial for outcome in patients with septic shock, ARDS, heart failure, acute brain injury, and out of hospital cardiac arrest, but not in patients with non-severe infection, undertreated infection, or infection in the central nervous system.

Price and McGloin [55] claim that for every patient in an ICU with elevated temperature, without exception, external cooling is required to reduce their temperature. Lee et al. [49] found that external cooling was not associated with increased mortality in critically ill patients. Others [56] reported a seven-fold higher mortality in non-neurological trauma patients with temperatures of greater than 38.5 °C (101.3 °F) who received aggressive fever management compared to those receiving a more permissive treatment at temperatures of more than 40 °C (104.0 °F). Others conclude that due to limited evidence, management of elevated temperature in ICUs is based to a large degree on rituals, and they recommend paracetamol in the first instance and question the use of fans [57]. Thompson et al. [37, 58] conclude that nurses in neuro ICU, in spite of knowledge of the negative consequences, do not follow prescribed guidelines in order to lower body temperature in traumatic brain injury. Kiekkas et al. [39], on the other hand, claim the present practice of aggressively and routinely lowering temperature in fever is not in line with current evidence-based knowledge.

Reflect on antipyresis in critically ill patients
Reflect on the site of measurement in critically ill patients.

Fever in Frail, Elderly Individuals

A vulnerable group are frail elderly individuals with cognitive and physical decline. In this population, the signs and symptoms of infection are often atypical, while specific symptoms may be missing, which can cause delays in diagnosis and treatment. Also, the complexity of detecting infections in nursing-home residents (NHR) is complicated by co-existing chronic diseases which confuse the clinical picture. Examples of atypical signs and symptoms are absence of increased body temperature assessed as fever, decline in general health, and decline in functional status, such as weakness, falling, deteriorating mobility, reduced food intake, weight loss, physical dysfunction, and new or increasing confusion [59–62]. In NHR with pneumonia, the presence of cognitive decline (50%) was as common as symptoms more specific to respiratory tract infection, such as cough and sputum production [63]. Caregivers, in the first-place nursing assistants, become the spokespersons for the frail elderly when they themselves cannot express feelings of discomfort and malaise. It seems as if the metaphoric expression 'he/she is not feeling well today', indicating the presence or the absence of a behavior is in itself sufficient information to trigger further action. These behaviors include confusion, aggressiveness, infirmity or apathy, unrestrained behavior, restlessness, changed food intake, pain, or expression in the eyes, and general signs and symptoms of illness [61, 62, 64].

As atypical signs and symptoms are common in frail elderly individuals, increased body temperature becomes an important sign of infection and is in fact crucial for even considering that they may be infected. However, it has long been known that the elderly may lack fever. Hippocrates drew the erroneous conclusion that 'fevers are not so acute in old people for then the body is cold' [65]. Today, research indicates that subgroups of elderly individuals might have a lower baseline body temperature due to age-related changes and frailty [66, 67]. A lower temperature in fever due to a lower baseline body temperature, when combined with co-morbidity and a delayed immunological response, can contribute to delayed diagnosis and therapy and thus to mortality [61, 62, 68]. Tingström et al. [61] found that a mean difference in increase of 1.6 °C ± 1.0 °C (34.9 °F ± 33.8 °F) from the baseline was strongly correlated to verified infection in frail nursing-home residents. Hence, with elderly individuals, it is wise to establish the individual morning body temperature on admission to the nursing-home facility and to use DiffTemp™ as a basis for assessing body temperature as fever [60]. Furthermore, pain is common in elderly individuals probably caused by chronic low-grade inflammation (see Chap. 8) [38]. This is associated with increased circulating levels of IL-6 and a constantly activated immune response, including elevated body temperature [69]. Due to pain, elderly individuals are often on daily medication with paracetamol, which lowers body temperature in fever and blurs assessment of suspected, ongoing infections.

Reflect on antipyresis in frail elderly individuals
Reflect on the site of measurement in frail elderly individuals with cognitive decline

Fever in Children

Fever is one of the most common reasons for parents to get in contact with health care professionals. For example, it is the main complaint in approximately 30% of patients consulting pediatricians [70–73] and can present pediatricians and caregivers with a diagnostic challenge. Infants with elevated body temperature are at risk of serious bacterial infections including bacteremia, meningitis, urinary tract infections, and pneumonia. One of the most common daily problems faced by the emergency physician is the management of the febrile child. It is important to identify which child is at risk of serious bacterial infection and what the key markers are. Even children who appear to be well may still have a serious illness, especially at an early stage when severity is not apparent, and may deteriorate rapidly [74]. In children below the age of 5 years presenting at the emergency department with fever but without specific signs, physicians might underestimate the likelihood of serious bacterial infection [75]. However, their caregivers act as voices for them as they compare changes in behavior from normal and make a proper judgment on the severity of the child's illness [72]. Mothers associate fever with specific changes in their child's normal behavior, such as lethargy, agitation or restlessness, irritability, listlessness, withdrawal, wanting to be comforted or staying close to the parent, refusing food, and babbling or becoming unusually quiet [76]. According to guidelines from child medical associations, parents should be advised to assess the child's activity level, look for signs of serious illness, and encourage fluid intake to facilitate hydration [71].

Mothers perceive fever as something good and a warning that something is 'going on'. On the other hand, mothers consider high fever, defined as above 38 °C (100.4 °F), as harmful and had to be treated, without concerns about the adverse effects of antipyretics. Beliefs about harm from high temperature in fever, ranging from 38 °C (100.4 °F) to 39 °C (102.2 °F), included fear of febrile convulsions, death, dehydration, stroke, and cardiac problems. Experiences which increased concerns about temperature in fever included febrile seizures, negative media reports, not receiving a definite diagnosis, inaccessibility of a familiar physician, conflicting information about fever management [76], and when the physician was worried about the fever [77]. However, parents' positive experiences reduced their concerns about increased body temperature in fever [76].

Misconception of increased body temperature assessed as fever, and the fear of it, are most likely also affected by the attitudes of the health care workers parents meet, especially nurses and physicians. For example, about 38% of pediatric nurses had insufficient physiological knowledge about fever and 83% had poor knowledge about the adverse effects of antipyretics. In line with parents, pediatric nurses appreciated the adaptive value of fever and knew that external cooling triggers shivering. In spite of this, pediatric nurses and physicians believe that it is necessary to reduce increased body temperature with antipyretics to prevent febrile seizures and based decisions about treatment on temperature and not a complete picture of the patient's condition [70, 71, 78]. Crocetti et al. [77] found that 91% of caregivers thought that increased body temperature assessed as fever could cause harmful effects, such as brain injury and death, and that the temperature could rise to above 43.4 °C (110.1 °F). They also reported that 85% would awaken the child to give antipyretics and that 73% sponged their child using cold water or alcohol. A Canadian study showed that 21.6% of parents controlled the temperature of the child as often as every 30–60 minutes when the child had a fever. Ninety percent of the parents always tried to lower the temperature with antipyretics and surface cooling [79].

In the 1990s, 70% of nurses and 30% of physicians routinely used drugs to lower increased body temperature in children. The rationale for antipyretics was the risk of febrile seizures in children [80]. In a recent study, only 15% of primary care physicians, in line with the updated guidelines [13], prescribed antipyretics to ensure the child's comfort and remove irritability [70]. However, about 70% of the physicians in this study also agreed that brain damage, seizures, and death are complications to fever, that temperature above 38 °C (100.4 °F) should always be treated with antipyretics and physical methods, and that antipyretics prevent febrile seizures. Of special concern is that physicians often advise caregivers to alternate ibuprofen and paracetamol in spite of the increased risk of overdosing and adverse effects [13, 70, 81].

In the early 1980s the concept 'fever phobia' was established, describing the unrealistic concerns about increased body temperature in febrile children [77]. This phobia, in terms of attitudes toward fever and reliance on antipyretics to reduce it and prevent seizures, still seem to persist among caregivers as well as within health care. Considering that pediatricians and nurses are the primary source for parents' understanding and ideas about temperature in fever [81], they have an important role in changing current misconceptions and in framing evidence-based management.

Reflect on the consequences of fever phobia.

Antipyresis in Children

Paracetamol, aspirin, and ibuprofen are commonly used drugs for lowering temperature in children with fever. Except for lowering temperature in fever, paracetamol is also commonly used by parents when children have headache or abdominal pain and discomfort [82], as well as for preventing febrile seizures [83]. However, these drugs have severe toxic effects. Paracetamol is associated with liver failure, disorders of the kidneys, heart, and effects on the blood cells and metabolism. It is also the most common pharmacological agent involved in overdose, especially in children under 6 years of age [82]. In addition, the toxicological effects of paracetamol are increased in conditions of anorexia, starving, and fever response [80]. Aspirin is also reported to cause metabolic acidosis, very low blood glucose, lethargy, and coma, and increases the risk of Reye's syndrome, a severe condition that may cause coma and death in children. Other reported complications with antipyretic drugs are gastrointestinal bleeding, nausea, vomiting dyspepsia, and heartburn [84]. Hence, such drugs should be avoided with children. It is also estimated that 50% of caregivers either give too low or too high a dose of the drug, or they give the medication more frequently than recommended, or alternate the antipyretic drugs given to the feverish child. This increases the risks of poisoning and adverse effects from the drugs [10, 71].

As for adults, physical methods, such as tepid sponging, bathing, fans, and cooling blankets, are commonly recommended by health care staff to parents. Common adverse effects of these physical methods are shivering, discomfort, and crying. Also, sponging with cool water may cause peripheral vasoconstriction and conservation instead of dissipation of body heat [85]. Systematic reviews report weak evidence for reducing fever in children, aged between 1 month and 15 years, with either paracetamol or physical methods alone or with paracetamol in combination with tepid sponging [29, 84–86]. The essential point is that interventions are induced to reduce the child's comfort and to support the body's response to infection. The focus should be on the child and the parents not the thermometer [86].

Febrile Seizures

Of special importance is to handle the caregivers' fear of febrile seizures, which are a revolutionary experience where it is common for the parents to believe that the child will die [87]. Approximately 2–5% of children have febrile seizures during the first 5 years of life. About one-third of these will have another febrile seizures and 10% have three or more [88, 89]. A febrile seizure is defined as a convulsion that occurs with a body temperature >38 °C (100.4 F) in the absence of intracranial infection, metabolic disturbance, or history of afebrile seizures [90]. The seizures are classified as simple or complex. The simple seizure, representing 65–90% of cases, is characterized by a duration of less than 15 minutes, is generalized in nature, and comprises a single occurrence during a period of 24 hours without previous neurological problems. A complex seizure, 10–35% of cases, has a duration of more than 15 minutes, is focal, and recurs within 24 hours [80, 83]. Febrile seizures can occur with virtually all infections that cause fever, for example, otitis and urinary tract infections and even after vaccinations [88]. The causes of febrile seizures are not fully understood [91]. However, there are suggestions of risk factors, such as developmental delay, discharge from neonatal unit after 28 days, daycare attendance, viral infections, some vaccinations, genetic predisposition, and iron and zinc deficiencies [83]. The most constant predictive factor seems to be age at onset, with 50% of children less than 12 months and 30% of children aged more than 12 months presenting with a recurrent febrile seizure. Nevertheless, simple febrile seizures are not dangerous and do not cause persisting neurological effects [91]. Neither antipyretics nor anticonvulsants are recommended for preventing febrile seizures due to lack of evidence and, in the latter, the risk of adverse effects [80, 83].

What's the focus—the child or the thermometer?

Hyperthermia

It is important to separate increased body temperature assessed as fever from hyperthermia as the underlying mechanisms differ, as do the options for treatment [55]. For example, in one study, registered nurses caring for patients with neurological insults did not differentiate between heat stroke and fever [27], which might have a high impact on ideas about managing elevated temperature in fever. As described in Chap. 6, the febrile response is a process, of which fever in terms of elevated body temperature is but one component, when the hypothalamus increases the core body temperature set point in response to agents which are recognized as foreign by the immune cells (see Chap. 6). It is of clinical importance that antipyretics lower the increased temperature related to fever by reducing the hypothalamic set point. In hyperthermia pyrogenic cytokines are not directly involved since the hypothalamus set point is altered, and so antipyretics have no effect on the elevated body temperature [92, 93]. Heat stroke is a serious problem during heatwaves, affecting, above all, the elderly and small children. For example, during the heat wave in Europe in August 2003, 29% of the almost 1500 victims were diagnosed as having heatstroke, hyperthermia, or dehydration. The treatment of hyperthermia aims to promote effective dissipation of heat by increasing the temperature gradient (conduction) and the water vapor pressure (evaporation) between the skin and the surrounding air, as well as the velocity of the air (see Chap. 5).

Based on these thermoregulatory principles and individual conditions, the recommended treatments are rapid cooling with whole body immersion in cold circulating water or spraying cool water continuously while fanning, utilizing as large a body area as possible. Immersion in iced water, started within minutes of the onset of exertional heat stroke, has been found to be effective and safe in young, healthy, and well-trained military personnel or athletes. However, for elderly individuals suffering from classic heat stroke, the technique was poorly tolerated and was associated with increased morbidity and mortality. For elderly individuals, non-invasive cooling modalities, such as ice packs or cold packs, wet gauze sheets, a fan alone or in combination, are reasonable alternatives when a frail, elderly patient is presenting with heat stroke. In general, antipyretic agents, such as aspirin and paracetamol, are not yet properly assessed for the treatment of heat stroke and should be avoided because of their potential to aggravate the coagulopathy and liver injury of heat stroke. Although rapid and effective cooling is the cornerstone of treatment, the management of circulatory failure in heat stroke is also important. Fluid replacement should be administered along with vasoactive drugs to restore blood pressure. Bouchama et al. also recommend that the therapeutic approach for hemodynamic management of sepsis can be applied to heatstroke because of the pathophysiological similarities between the two diseases [94].

In small children the most imminent risk for heatstroke is associated with situations in which a hot environment prevents necessary heat dissipation. An example is the classical situation when a sleeping child is left in the car, while the caregivers carry out some errands. When they return to the car, they find the child unconscious. Even on a cloudy and/or not so hot day, the temperature within a car might become dangerous to animals and humans.

There are various human thermal comfort indices that can be used to predict the possibility of heat-related stress and illness. Figure 9.3 presents a compilation of indices in relation to outside air temperature, time for rise in both air and radiation temperature inside a car on a sunny day in July 2018 in Stockholm, Sweden. The figure shows that the interior of the vehicle had reached a dangerously high temperature within a 30-minute period and ought to be considered a life-threatening environment (Fig. 9.3) (see Chap. 5).

Reflect on radiation, convection, conduction, and evaporation when the temperature rises inside a car.

Hypothermia

Accidental hypothermia outside hospital care is described more in Chap. 5. In clinical practice, hypothermia is related to surgical procedures and postoperative care. Prevention of hypothermia in order to maintain normothermia should span the period of the surgery as well as the perioperative and postoperative periods [95]. It is also important when talking about achieving normothermia postoperatively that the patient's temperature is compared to their individual baseline temperature measured preoperatively [96].

General anesthesia obliterates normal heat-regulating compensation mechanisms which omit the body to the ambient temperature. Perioperative hypothermia is the most common heat disorder during anesthesia and is due to a combination of impaired heat regulation, that is, redistribution of

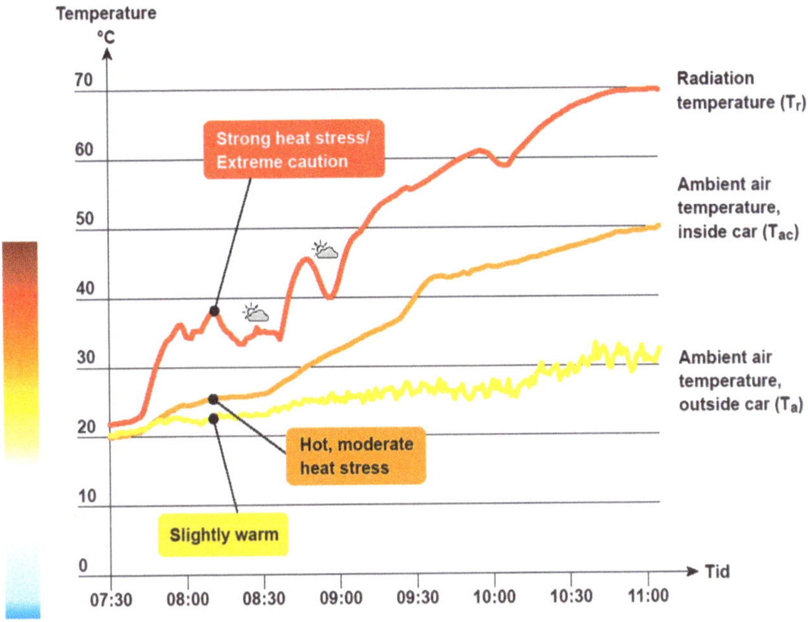

Fig. 9.3 Predictive heat-related stress in an enclosed vehicle. Temperatures within a car related to outdoor temperature and weather. 70 °C (158 °F); 60 °C (140 °F); 50 °C (122 °F); 40 °C (104 °F); 30 °C (8.6 °F); 20 °C (68 °F); 10 °C (50 °F). Tac temperature ambient car, Ta temperature ambient, Tr temperature radiant. (With permission from Rosita Christensen, Karolinska Institute Sweden)

heat to the peripheral parts of the body, as well as anesthetics, exposure to a cold operating environment, cold intravenous fluids, and blood products [97–100]. Perioperative hypothermia is related to several adverse outcomes, such as decreased metabolic rate and cardiac output, metabolic acidosis, prolongation of muscle relaxants, altered clotting functions, postoperative infection, postoperative shivering, extended length of hospital stay, and mortality [96, 100–102]. Patients at risk of perioperative hypothermia include especially frail elderly individuals and children, as well as patients with cachexia, burn injuries, and hypothyroidism [102]. To prevent perioperative hypothermia, active warming is suggested for all individuals with a core temperature of less than 36 °C (96.8 °F), though the recommendation for what is considered to be the core temperature varies in clinical guidelines [103, 104].

Postoperative hypothermia is present in approximately 50–70% of patients who undergo surgery lasting 2 hours or more [98]. During the postoperative phase, normothermia is essential for optimal patient outcome [104, 105]. Before discharge from postoperative care, the patients' temperature should be 36 °C (96.8 °F) or more [104]. During postoperative care recommended preoperative warming are the so-called active methods, such as forced-air warming blankets, carbon fiber blankets, and conductive carbon polymer mattresses [96, 100, 102, 103]. Warming is cost-effective if it is used in procedures that exceed 30 minutes. A combination of preoperative warming commencement and the use of warm fluids and forced-air warming is recommended for vulnerable patients, such as elderly individuals, and in patients undergoing long surgeries [101]. In addition, the benefits of warming the patient include decreased shivering and blood loss, earlier extubation, and increased thermal comfort.

Therapeutic Hypothermia

In order to prevent cerebral ischemia during surgery and postoperatively, therapeutic hypothermia has been used since the 1960s in traumatic brain injury [37]. Elevated temperature during the acute phase of the trauma is associated with longer stays in the neuro intensive care unit (NICU), increased intracranial pressure, unconsciousness, poor functional status, increased excitatory amino acid release and metabolic demands, and intracerebral edema [106]. The rationale for therapeutic hypothermia is to improve the oxygen supply to ischemic areas of the brain and to decrease intracranial pressure. Recent research in traumatic brain injury, subarachnoid hemorrhage, ischemic stroke, and meningitis have failed to demonstrate a significant outcome benefit [107].

There is no consensus on methods for therapeutic hypothermia, but surface cooling with alcohol, circulating cold water, or forced cold air blankets, cold-water immersion, icepacks, and invasive cooling with cold fluids are the most common procedures. A national survey of NICUs in the United States found that the cut-off value for starting actions to lower body temperature in traumatic brain injury varied between 37 °C (98.6 °F) and 40 °C (104.0 °F) [37]. In addition, reliable temperature measurement is essential, for example, the rectal site is not recommended due to fecal insulation [108] and a serious lag time to adjust to hypothalamus set-point temperature (see Chap. 7).

Serious immediate side-effects with external cooling are shivering, hypovolemia, hypotension, electrolyte disorders, coagulopathy, and hyperglycemia, especially in the induction phase. Shivering causes great strain in terms of increased metabolic demands, increased oxygen consumption, vasoconstriction, vasospasm of the coronary arteries, and rebound hypothermia [52, 107, 108]. Hence, sedation and neuromuscular blockage are crucial during induced hypothermia. Rewarming after induced hypothermia is also critical because when constricted peripheral vascular beds start to dilate and the circulation of cooler blood from the core to the extremities increases the risk of hypotension occurring. It is, therefore, important to continue to support arterial pressure during this period.

However, studies contradict each other about the benefits of hypothermia for patients with cerebral injuries. Mayor Basto et al. [9] conclude that therapeutic hypothermia is an extremely powerful neuroprotectant and is the most promising treatment for patients with acute ischemic stroke. It preserves neuronal vitality by modulating several metabolic pathways, inflammation, apoptosis, and preservation of the neurovascular unit [109]. Others question if hypothermia after acute injury actually protects the brain from poor outcome in terms of severe disability, vegetative state, or death [110, 111]. Rincon [107] reported that recent research in traumatic brain injury, subarachnoid hemorrhage, ischemic stroke, and meningitis have failed to demonstrate a significant outcome benefit [107]. Kiekkas et al. [52] concludes that, although a consensus on the need for cerebral hypothermia in cerebral trauma patients is lacking, maintaining core temperature within the normal range of 36.5 °C (97.7 °F) to 37.5 ° C (99.5 °F) seems to be the best choice. A recent randomized trial reported that among patients with severe traumatic brain injury, early prophylactic hypothermia compared with normothermia did not improve neurologic outcomes at 6 months [112]. This is supported in a systematic Cochrane review concluding that there is no evidence that hypothermia for neuroprotection during brain surgery is effective compared with normothermia [113]. Another systematic review found that some methods of head cooling can reduce intracranial pressure, but there is insufficient evidence to recommend it outside of research trials [95]. In the last decade hypothermia also has been introduced as a protective measure after cardiac arrest. Unlike brain injury, there is a consensus about the clinical effects of lowering body temperature in such cases. Therapeutic hypothermia have been showed to be neuroprotective and significantly reduce mortality and benefit long-term functional outcome in cardiac arrest [107]. All adult patients who have return of spontaneous circulation and remain unconscious following cardiac arrest should be cooled to between 32 °C (89.6 °F) and 34 °C (93.2 °F) for at least 12 to 24 hours [110].

Consider 'normothermia' in cases where the baseline body temperature is low, such as in frail, elderly patients?
Reflect on the site of measurement and rewarming after hypothermia.

Practical Guidelines When Assessing Body Temperature

When assessing body temperature, it is essential to remember that temperatures outside the hypothalamus are themselves estimates of the core temperature and have their own variability. Simply adding an offset assuming that the differences between different sites and methods are linear does not take thermoregulation and the complexity of the human body into consideration [114]. Because of the different thermal influences and profiles, a lack of agreement between measurements does not necessarily mean that one site is true and the other false [115]. However, this is often the conclusion in studies of body temperature measurement. For example, a worldwide cited systematic review found deviations between the ear and rectal temperatures in children and concluded that the ear site is not an acceptable approximation of rectal temperature [75]. Another study reported large variations in simultaneously measured non-adjusted rectal, oral, ear, and axillary temperatures in healthy adult subjects and interpreted this as a natural variation. The authors conclude that in order to improve evaluation of body temperature, the assessment should be based on individual variation, the same site of measurement, and no adjustment between sites [116]. These differing ways of interpreting results have a great impact on the assessment of body temperature in clinical practice. Hence, the use of rectal temperature as a reference may result in the ear reading being dismissed as an inaccurate and insensitive method for detecting fever, when in fact the readings may reflect the fact that defervesce has already occurred, thus resulting in a lower ear temperature being recorded while the rectal temperature remains high [117]. Also, as medication with analgesics is common in elderly individuals and antipyretics are frequently used in febrile patients [3], the low reading may be due to antipyretics affecting the ear temperature while the rectal temperature remains elevated [19]. (See Fig. 9.2).

As the range of body temperatures is wider than traditionally asserted and varies with different conditions, such as physical and cognitive decline, gender, and the site of measurement, body temperature should be evaluated in relation to individual variability. A baseline value should be taken. The best approach is to use the same site without adjustments to other sites. As normal body temperature shows individual variation, it is reasonable that the same should hold true for increased body temperature assessed as fever [18]. Therefore, instead of a fixed cut-off value, fever should be assessed as an increase of at least 1 °C (33.8 °F) from the individual baseline body temperature, Diff Temp™, in combination with malaise [20].

In summary, assessment of body temperature should be based on scientific knowledge instead of ancient tradition and personal beliefs. In order to promote evidence-based practice, the following should be the basis on which to assess body temperature [9].

Evaluate body temperature in relation to the individual baseline temperature.

In frail, elderly residents, the baseline temperature may be altered due to functional and cognitive impairment, loss of insulating tissue, and chronic pain.

As far as possible, an individual baseline body temperature should be recorded, at least in the nursing home.

The axillary or forehead site is not recommendable for an assessment of core body temperature in adolescents and adults.

The unadjusted mode of the thermometer should be used without adjusting to another site.

Use correct operator technique when measuring body temperature.

The same site of measurement should be always used, or as far as is possible.

Time, site of measurement, and medication antipyretics should be noted in the patient record.

Reflections

- Reflect on the use of antipyretics when your child is feverish.
- Reflect on antipyretics when a frail, elderly person expresses feelings of malaise.
- Reflect on different measuring sites, such as rectal vs. ear, oral, etc.
- Reflect on education in operator technique when measuring body temperature.

References

1. Thompson H. Fever: a concept analysis. J Adv Nurs. 2004;51(5):484–92.
2. Hasday J, Ahah N, Mackowiak P, Tulapurkar M, Nagarsekar A, Singh I. Fever, hyperthermia, and the lungs: it's all about context and timing. Trans Am Clin Climatol Assoc. 2011;122:34–47.
3. Mackowiak PA. Physiological rationale for suppression of fever. Clin Infect Dis. 2000;31(Suppl. 5):185–9.
4. Kozak W. Regulated decreases in body temperature. In: Mackowiak PA, editor. Fever basic mechanisms and management. 2nd ed. Philadelphia: Lippincott Raven; 1997. p. 467–87.
5. Kluger M. The adaptive value of fever. In: Mackowiak PA, editor. Fever basic mechanisms and management. 2nd ed. Philadelphia: Lippincott Raven; 1997. p. 255–66.
6. Kushimoto S, Gando S, Saitoh C, Mayumi T, Ogura H, Fujishima S, et al. The impact of body temperature abnormalities on the disease severity and outcome in patients with severe sepsis: an analysis from a multicenter prospective survey of severe sepsis. Crit Care. 2013;17(R271):1–9.
7. Mackowiak P. What do we do when we suppress fever. Curr Infect Dis Rep. 2005;7:1–4.
8. Launey Y, Nesseler N, Malle'dant Y, Seguin P. Clinical review: fever in septic ICU patients_ friend or foe? Crit Care. 2011;15(222):1–7.
9. Sund Levander M, Grodzinsky E. Time for a change to assess and evaluate body temperature in clinical practice. Int J Nurs Pract. 2009;15:241–9.
10. Pereira G, Tavares N, Mengue S, Dal Pizzol T. Therapeutic procedures and use of alternating antipyretic drugs for fever management in children. J Pediatr. 2013;89(1):25–32.
11. Niven D, Laupland K, Tabah A, Vesin A, Rello J, Koulenti D, et al. Diagnosis and management of temperature abnormality in ICUs: a EUROBACT investigators' survey. Crit Care. 2013;17(R289):1–8.
12. Chen ZM, Zhiang XB, Li Long, M, Yu Pu M. Accuracy of infrared ear thermometry in children: a meta-analysis and systematic review. Clin Pediatr. 2014;53:1158–65.
13. Chiappin E, Venturini E, Remaschi G, Principi N, Longhi R, Tovo P, et al. 2016 update of the Italian pediatric society guidelines for management of fever in children. J Pediatr. 2017;180:177–83.
14. Geijer H, Udumyan R, Lohse G, Nilsagard Y. Temperature measurements with a temporal scanner: systematic review and meta-analysis. BMJ Open [Internet]. 2016; 6:e009509.
15. Kiekkas P, Stefanopouluus S, Bakalis N, Kefaliakois A, Karanikolas M. Agreement of infrared temporal artery thermometry with other thermometry methods in adults: systematic review. J Clin Nurs. 2016;25:894–905.

16. Niven D, Gaudet J, Laupland K, Mrklas K, Roberts D, Stelfox H. Accuracy of peripheral thermometers for estimating temperature: a systematic review and meta-analysis. Ann Intern Med. 2015;163:768–77.
17. Scrase W, Tranter S. Improving evidence-based care for patients with pyrexia. Nurs Stand. 2011;25(29):37–41.
18. Mackowiak PA. Fever's upper limit. In: Mackowiak PA, editor. Fever basic mechanisms and management. 2nd ed. Philadelphia: Lippincott Raven; 1997. p. 147–63.
19. Sund Levander M, Tingtröm P. Fever or not fever – that's the question: a cohort study of simultaneously measured rectal and ear temperatures in febrile patients with suspected infection. Clin Nurs Stud. 2018;6(2):48–54.
20. Sund Levander M, Grodzinsky E. Variation in normal ear temperature. Am J Med Sci. 2017;354(4):370–8.
21. DuBois EF. The many different temperatures of the human body and its parts. West J Surg. 1951;59:476–90.
22. Ring EFJ, McEvoy H, Jungs A, Ubers J, Nachin M. New standards for devices used for the measurement of human body temperature. J Med Eng Technol. 2010;34(4):249–53.
23. Geijer H, Udumyan R, Lohse G, Nilsagard Y. Temperature measurements with a temporal scanner: systematic review and meta-analysis. BMJ Open. 2016;6(3):e009509.
24. Stolpe S. I dödens väntrum (In the waiting room of death). Stockholm: Libris; 1930.
25. Legget J. Approach to fever or suspected infection in the normal host. In: Goldman LS, Schafer AI, editors. Goldman's Cecil Medicine. 24th ed. Philadelphia: Elsevier Saunders; 2011. p. 64.
26. Ames N, Peng C, Powers J, Kline Leidy N, Miller-Davis C, Rosenberg A, et al. Beyond intuition: patient fever symptom experience. J Pain Symptom Manage. 2013;46(6):1–14.
27. Thompson H, Kagan S. Clinical management of fever by nurses: doing what works. J Adv Nurs. 2010;67(2):359–70.
28. Grossman D, Keen MF, Singer M, Asher M. Current nursing practices in fever management. Medsurg Nurs. 1995;4(3):193–8.
29. Sund Levander M, Wahren LK, Hamrin E. Nursing care in fever: assessment and implementation. Vård i Norden. 1998;18(2):27–30.
30. Kasting NW. A rationale for centuries of therapeutic bloodletting: antipyretic therapy for febrile illness. Perspect Biol Med. 1990;33(4):509–16.
31. Aiygari V, Diringer M. Fever control and its impact on outcomes: what is the evidence? J Neurol Sci. 2007;261:39–46.
32. Mackwiak P. Diagnostic implications and clinical consequences of antipyretic therapy. Clin Infect Dis. 2000;31:230–3.

33. Chan E, Chen W. External cooling methods for treatment of fever in adults: a systematic review. JBI Libr Syst Rev. 2010;8(20):793–825.
34. Carey J. Literature review: should antipyretic therapies routinely be administrated to patient fever? J Clin Nurs. 2010;19:2377–93.
35. Emilsson M, Sanden I. Nurses caring for adult patients with fever. In Swedish Vård i Norden. 2007;83(27):37–42.
36. Mackowiak PA. Benefits versus risks of the febrile response. In: Mackowiak PA, editor. Fever basic mechanisms and management. 2nd ed. Philadelphia: Lippincott Raven; 1997. p. 279–86.
37. Thompson H, Kirkness C, Mitchell P. Fever management practice of neuroscience nurses, part II: nurse, patient, and barriers. J Neurosci Nurs. 2007;39(4):196–201.
38. Axelrod P. External cooling in the management of fever. Clin Infect Dis. 2000;31(Suppl 5):S224–9.
39. Kiekkas P, Diamanto A, Bakalis N, Karpouhtsi I, Marneras C, Baltopoulus G. Fever effects and treatment in critical care: literature review. Aust Crit Care. 2012;26:130–5.
40. Van Someren E, Raymann R, Scherder E, Daanen H, Swaab D. Circadian and age-related modulation of thermoreception and temperature regulation: mechanisms and functional implications. Ageing Res Rev. 2002;1(4):721–78.
41. Guyton A, Hall J. Body temperature, temperature regulation and fever. In: Guyton AC, Hall JE, editors. Textbook of medical physiology. 13th ed. Philadelphia: W. B. Saunders Company; 2012. p. 822–33.
42. Holtzclaw BJ. Shivering: a clinical nursing problem. Nurs Clin North Am. 1990;25(4):976–86.
43. Sund Levander M, Wahren LK. Assessment and prevention of shivering in patients with severe cerebral injury. A pilot study. J Clin Nurs. 2000;9:55–61.
44. Mackowiak PA. Clinical thermometric measurements. In: Mackowiak PA, editor. Fever basic mechanisms and management. 2nd ed. Philadelphia: Lippincott Raven; 1997. p. 27–33.
45. Mackowiak P. Antipyretic therapy future. Clin Infect Dis. 2000;31:242–3.
46. Loke A, Chan H, Chan T. Comparing the effectiveness of two types of cooling blankets for febrile patients. Nurs Crit Care. 2005;10(5):247–54.
47. Doyle J, Schortgren F. Should we treat pyrexia? And how do we do it? Crit Care [Internet]. 2016;20:1–10.
48. Niven D, Laupland K. Pharmacotherapy of fever control among hospitalizes adult patients. Expert Opin Pharmacother. 2013;14:735–45.
49. Lee H, Inui D, Suh G, Kim J, Kwon J, Park J, et al. Association of body temperature and antipyretic treatments with mortality of critically ill patients with and without sepsis: multi-centered prospective observational study. Crit Care. 2012;16(R33):1–13.

50. Neto A, Pereria V, Colomco G, De la Cruq SF, Pessoa C, Rocha L. Should we treat fever in critically ill patients? A summary of the current evidence from three randomized controlled trials. Einstein. 2014;12:518–23.
51. Celik S, Yildirim I, Arslan I, Yamashita S, Erdal F, Yandi Y. Hemodynamic and oxynenation changes in surgical intensive unit patients with fever and fever lowering nursing interventions. Int J Nurs Pract. 2011;17:556–61.
52. Kiekkas P, Brokalaki H, Manolis E, Askotiri P, Karga M, Baltopoulus G. Fever and standard monitoring parameters of ICU patients: a descriptive study. Intensive Crit Care Nurs. 2007;23:281–8.
53. Niven D, Stelfox H, Laupland K. Antipyretic therapy in febrile critically ill adults: a systematic review and meta-analysis. J Crit Care. 2013;28:303–10.
54. Doyle FD, Zehner J, Terndrup TE. The effect of ambient temperature extremes on tympanic and oral temperatures. Am J Emerg Med. 1992;10(4):285–9.
55. Price T, McGloin S. A review of cooling patients with severs cerebral insult in ICU (part 1). Nurs Crit Care. 2003;8(1):30–6.
56. Schulman C, Namias N, Doherty J, Manning R, Elhaddad A, Lasko D, et al. The effects of antipyretic therapy upon outcomes in critically ill patients: a randomised, prospective study. Surg Infect. 2005;6(4):369–75.
57. Prado G, McGloin S, Gilchrist M. Cooling strategies for patients with severe cerebral insult in ICU (part 2). Nurs Crit Care. 2003;8(1):37–45.
58. Thompson H, Kirkness C, Mitchell P. Intensive care unit management of fever following traumatic brain injury. Intensive Crit Care Nur. 2007;23:91–6.
59. High K, Bradley S, Gravenstein S, Mehr D, Quagliarello V, Richards C, et al. Clinical practice guideline for the evaluation of fever and infection in older adult residents of long-term care facilities: 2008 update by the Infectious Diseases Society of America. Clin Infect Dis. 2009;48(2):149–71.
60. Sund Levander M, Grodzinsky E. The challenge of infections in frail elderly: The story of Mr Nilsson. Clin Med Rev Case Rep. 2015;2(9):1–2.
61. Tingström P, Milberg A, Rodhe N, Ernerud J, Grodzinsky E, Sund Levander M. "He seems to be ill"- a reason for nurses to take action: validation of the early detection scale of infection (EDIS). BMC Geriatr. 2015;15(122):1–10.
62. Tingström P, Milberg A, Sund Levander M. Early nonspecific signs and symptoms of infection in institutionalized elderly persons: perceptions of nursing assistants. Scand J Nurs Sci. 2010;24:24–31.
63. Sund Levander M, Örtqvist Å, Grodzinsky E, Klefsgård Ö, Wahren LK. Morbidity, mortality and clinical presentation of nursing home- acquired pneumonia in a Swedish population. Scand J Infect Dis. 2003;35:306–10.
64. Allemann H, Sund Levander M. Nurses' actions in response to nursing assistants' observations of signs and symptoms of infections among nursing home residents. Nurs Open. 2015;2(3):97–104.
65. Guly H. History of accidental hypothermia. Resuscitation. 2011;82:122–5.

66. Bender SB, Scarpace PJ. Fever in the elderly. In: Mackowiak PA, editor. Fever basic mechanisms and management. 2nd ed. Philadelphia: Lippincott Raven; 1997. p. 363–73.
67. Sund Levander M, Wahren LK. The impact of ADL-status, dementia and body mass index on normal body temperature in elderly nursing home residents. Arch Gerontol Geriatr. 2002;35:161–9.
68. Roghmann M-C, Warner J, Mackowiak P. The relationship between age and fever magnitude. Am J Med Sci. 2001;322(2):68–70.
69. Bruunsgaard H, Pedersen M, Klarlund Pedersen BK. Aging and proinflammatory cytokines. Curr Opin Haematol. 2001;8:131–6.
70. Dermi F, Sekreter O. Knowledge, attitudes and misconceptions of primary care physicians regarding fever in children: a cross sectional study. Ital J Paediatr. 2012;38(40):1–7.
71. Hoover L. AAP reports on the use of antipyretics for fever in children. Am Fam Physician. 2012;1(85):518–9.
72. van Lerland A, Seiger N, van Veen M, Van Meurs A, Ruige M, Moll H. Self-referral and serious illness in children with fever. Pediatrics. 2012;129(3):e643–51.
73. Clarke P. Evidence-based management of childhood fever: what pediatric nurses need to know. J Pediatr Nurs. 2014;25:371–5.
74. Thompson M, Van den Bruel A, Verbakel J, Lakhanpaul M, Haj-Hassan T, Stevens R, et al. Systematic review and validation of prediction rules for identifying children with serious infections in emergency departments and urgent-access primary care. Health Technol Assess. 2012;16(15):1–100.
75. Crai GJ, Williams G, Jones M, Codarini M, Macaskill P, Hayen A, et al. The accuracy of clinical symptoms and signs for the diagnosis of serious bacterial infection in young febrile children. BMJ. 2010;340(20).
76. Walsh A, Edwards H, Fraser J. Influences of parents' fever management; beliefs, experiences and information sources. J Clin Nurs. 2006;16:2331–40.
77. Crocetti M, Moghbel N, Serwint J. Fever phobia revisited: have parental misconceptions about fever changed in 20 years? Pediatrics. 2001;107(6):1241–6.
78. Walsh A, Edwards H, Courtny M, Wilson E, Monaghan S. Fever management: paediatric nurses' knowledge, attitudes and influencing factors. Issues Innov Nurs Pract. 2005;49(5):453–64.
79. Enarso NM, Ali S, Vandermeer B, Wright R, Klassen T, Spiers J. Beliefs and expectations of Canadian parents who bring febrile children for medical care. Pediatrics. 2012;130:905–12.
80. Axelsson I. Feberkramper kan inte förebyggas (Febrile seizures cannot be prevented) In Swedish. Läkartidningen. 2010;19–20:290–1.
81. Chiappini E, Parretti A, Becherucci P, Perattelli M, Bonsignori F, Galli L, et al. Parental and medical knowledge and management of fever in Italian pre-school children. BioMed Cen Pediatr. 2012;12(97):3–10.

82. Obu H, Chinawa J, Ubesie A, Wke C, Ndu I. Paracetamol use (and misuse) in children in Enugu. South-East Niger BioMed Cen Pediatr. 2012;12(103):1–5.
83. Graves R, Oehler K, Tingle L. Febrile sezures: riska, evaluation and prognosis. Am Fam Physician. 2012;15(85):149–53.
84. Meremikwu M, Oyo-Ita A. Paracetamol for treating fever in children (review). Cochrane Database Syst Rev. 2002;2
85. Meremikwu M, Oyo-Ita A. Physical methods for treating fever in children (Review). The Cochrane Database of Systematic Reviews: Cochrane Database of Systematic Reviews; 2003. No.:CD004264.
86. Watts R, Robertson J, Thomas G. Nursing management of fever in children: a systematic review. Int J Nurs Pract. 2003;9:51–8.
87. Westin E, Sund Levander M. Parents' experiences of their children suffering febrile seizures. J Pediatr Nurs. 2018;38:68–73.
88. Kimia A, Bachur R, Torres A, Harper M. Febrile seizures: emergency medicine perspective. Curr Opin Pediatr 2015;27(3):292
89. Pavlidou EHC, Panteliadis C. Febrile seizures: recent developments and unanswered questions. Review. Childs Nerv Syst. 2013;29:2011–7.
90. AAP. Clinical practice guideline. Febrile seizures: guideline for the neurodiagnostic evaluation of the child with a simple febrile seizure. Pediatrics: American Academy of Pediatrics. Subcommittee on Febrile Seizures; 2011.
91. Mittal R. Recent advances in febrile seizures. Indian J Pediatr. 2014;81(9):909–16.
92. Musselman ME, Saely S. Diagnosis and treatment of drug-induced hyperthermia. Am J Health Syst Pharm. 2013;70:34–42.
93. Plaisance K, Mackowiak P. Antipyretic therapy. Arch Intern Med. 2000;160:449–56.
94. Bouchama A, Dehbi M, Chaves-Carballo E. Cooling and hemodynamic management in heatstroke: practical recommendations. Crit Care. 2007;11:R54(3):1–10.
95. Harris B, Andrews P, Murray G, Forbes J, Moseley O. Systematic review of head cooling in adults after traumatic brain injury and stroke. Health Technol Assess. 2012;16(45):1–44.
96. Bernard H. Patient warming in surgery and the enhanced recovery. Br J Nurs. 2013;2(6):19–25.
97. Fatemi S, Armat N, Zeydi E, Soleimani A, Kiabi F. Inadvertent perioperative hypothermia: a literature review of an old overlooked problem. Acta Facultatis Medicae Naissensis. 2016;33(1):5–11.
98. Ruetzler K, Kurz A, editors. Consequences of perioperative hypothermia. ScienceDirect; 2018. https://www.sciencedirect.com/journal/handbook-of-clinical-neurology/issues
99. Roopmans R, Ekkerink J, van Weel C. Survival to late dementia in Dutch nursing home patients. J Am Geriat Soc. 2003;51:184–7.

100. Roberson M, Dieckman L, Rodriguez R, Austin P. A review of the evidence for active preoperative warming of adults undergoing general anesthesia. Am Assoc Nurse Anesth. 2013;81(5):351–6.
101. Moola S, Lockwood C. The effectiveness of strategies for the management and/or prevention of hypothermia within the adult perioperative environment: systematic review. JBI Libr Syst Rev. 2010;8(19):752–92.
102. Warttig S, Alderson P, Campell G, Smith A. Interventions for treating inadequate postoperative hypothermia (Review). The Cochrane Database of Systematic Reviews: Cochrane Database of Systematic Reviews; 214. No.: CD009892. doi: 10.1002/14651858.CD009892.pub2.
103. Hardcastle T, Stander M, Kalafatis N, Hodgson R, Gopalan D. External patient temperature control in emergency centres, trauma centres, intensive care units and operating theatres: a multi-society literature review. Forum Clin Pract. 2013;103(9):609–11.
104. NICE. Hypothermia: prevention and management in adults having surgery. NICE guideline: National Institute for Health and Carre Excellences (NICE); 2016.
105. Philips N, Street M, Kent B, Cadeddu M. Determining criteria to assess patient readiness for discharge from postanaesthetic care: an international Delphi study. J Clin Nurs. 2014;23:3345–55.
106. Sharfique M, Shakir A, Baig M. The role of perioperative warming in surgery: a systematic review. Sao Paulo Med J. 2009;127:231–7.
107. Rincon F. Target temperature management in brain injured patients. Neurol Clin. 2018;29:231–53.
108. Baron J. Therapeutic hypothermia: implications for acute care practitioners. Postgrad Med. 2010;122:19–27.
109. Mayor Basto F, Lyden P. Hypothermia in acute ischemic stroke therapy. In: Romanovsky A, editor. Handbook of Clinical Neurology, Thermoregulation: Basic Neuroscience to Clinical Neurology, Part II. 157. Amsterdam: Elsevier; 2018. p. 823–37.
110. Collins TJ, Samworth P. Therapeutic hypothermia after cardiac arrest: a review of the evidence. Nurs Crit Care. 2008;13(3):141–51.
111. Greisman L, Mackowiak P. Fever: beneficial and detrimental effects of antipyretics. Curr Opin Infect Dis. 2002;15(3):241–5.
112. Cooper D, Nichol A, Bailey M, Bernard S, Cameron P, Pili-Floury S, et al. Effect of early sustained prophylactic hypothermia on neurologic outcomes among patients with severe traumatic brain injury: the POLAR randomized clinical trial. JAMA. 2018;320(21):2211–20.
113. Milani W, Antibas P, Prado G. Cooling for cerebral protection during brain surgery. Cochrane Database Syst Rev. 2011;(Oct):CD006638. doi: 10.1002/14651858.CD006638.pub2.
114. McCarthy P, Heusch A. The vagaries of ear temperature assessment. J Med Eng Technol. 2006;30(4):242–51.

115. Pursell E, While A, Coomber B. Tympanic thermometry- normal temperature and reliabolity. Paeditr Nurs. 2009;21(6):40–3.
116. Sund Levander M, Grodzinsky E, Loyd D, Wahren LK. Error in body temperature assessment related to individual variation, measuring technique and equipment. Int J Nurs Pract. 2004;10:216–23.
117. Chamberlain JM, Terndrup TE, Alexander DT, Silverstone FA, Wolf-Klein G, O'Donell R, et al. Determination of normal ear temperature with an infrared emission detection thermometer. Ann Emerg Med. 1995;25:15–20.

CHAPTER 10

Conclusions

Scenario 1

Imagine a hot summer day. You are going to the supermarket. On your way you observe a sleeping child in a car. The child's skin is red and you notice that no window is open.

- Reflect on heat dissipation.
- Reflect on hypermetabolic status.
- Reflect on the same situation, but for a middle-aged person or an elderly person with cognitive decline.

Scenario 2

A young woman visits the emergency department (ED) and describes malaise with high fever, shivering, a sore throat, joint pain, cough, headache and respiratory problems. She feels terribly ill. Two days earlier, she had called the ED and was advised to take painkillers and await developments. The nurse measures body temperature to be 36.4°C (97.5°F) and advises the patient to go home and contact her primary care centre the next day.

- Reflect on the definition of fever.
- Reflect on the measurement technique.
- Reflect on the role of painkillers.

E. Grodzinsky, M. Sund Levander (eds.), *Understanding Fever and Body Temperature*, https://doi.org/10.1007/978-3-030-21886-7_10

Scenario 3

The following are excerpts from the medical journal of a 93-year-old woman with severe dementia.

Day 1: Poor condition in the morning, pale, wheezing and restless. Legs and feet are warm. Rectal temperature 37.1°C (98.8°F). No fever.
Day 2: Difficulty in breathing, wheezing, cough. Temperature in the morning; In the ear 37.7°C (99.9°F) and rectum 38.3°C (100.9°F). Blood test: Interleukin-6: 400*. Pneumonia.
Day 3: The patient died in the morning.
*Normal value is <10.

- Reflect on the definition of fever.
- Reflect on the suspected infection in frail, elderly patients
- Reflect on the cytokines involved.

Scenario 4

A mother and her 12-year-old son visit the emergency department (ED) as the boy has bowel pain. The mother has measured a high fever, rectally, at home. The boy is discharged as no fever is recorded with an ear thermometer. Three hours later the boy undergoes an acute surgery because of an infected, ruptured appendix.

- Reflect on the definition of fever.
- Reflect on the measurement technique.
- Reflect on the role of painkillers.
- Reflect on acute-phase proteins.

Scenario 5

An old man is admitted to the hospital with pneumonia and assessed with high body temperature. You induce cooling with cold water, open the window and undress him. Half an hour later you notice that he is shivering severely.

- Reflect on the shivering and its consequences.
- Reflect on acute-phase proteins.
- Reflect on cytokines.

- Reflect on the immune response in the elderly.
- Reflect on antipyretics.
- Reflect on fever phases.

Scenario 6

Martha is working in her garden. Suddenly she feels a burning sting in her elbow. Six hours later she shivers and feels very ill.

- Reflect on delayed hypersensitive reactions.
- Reflect on the innate and adaptive immune systems.
- Reflect on the cytokines involved.
- Reflect on acute-phase proteins.

Scenario 7

Martin runs around in July out in the fields. When he comes home his nose is running and his eyes are itching.

- Reflect on allergic reactions.
- Reflect on immunoglobulins.
- Reflect on immune sensitization.
- Reflect on the innate and adaptive immune systems.
- Reflect on body temperature.

Scenario 8

Mrs. Benson, aged 45, presents with fatigue, weight loss and increased body temperature for several months. Now she feels worse and also describes increased photosensitivity when exposed to sunlight.

- Reflect on autoimmune disease and the immune-complex diseases.
- Reflect on the adaptive immune system.
- Reflect on acute-phase proteins.
- Reflect on auto-antibodies.

Scenario 9

James takes part in strenuous training for running a marathon. To enhance his future performance he included phases of short-term intensive training. He wonders why he always feels feverish after 5 minutes of intense training.

- Reflect on the reason for increased body temperature.
- Reflect on inflammatory response and muscle soreness.
- Reflect on the role of thermoregulation.
- Reflect on sudomotor control.

Scenario 10

Maria and Ewa are training for a triathlon. After a 3-day period of intensified running and cycling they wonder why muscle soreness has become worse after running.

- Reflect on functional overreaching and immune response.
- Reflect on acute-phase proteins.
- Reflect on the innate and adaptive immune response.
- Reflect on the value of assessing body temperature.

Scenario 11

Little Felicia and her schoolmate Karin both have chickenpox. Felicia's mother gives her paracetamol (acetaminophen) almost every day, while Karin's mother does not. When Karin comes back to school she heard that Felicia is still at home with spots.

- Reflect on the beneficial effects of fever.
- Reflect on antipyretic therapy and recovery.
- Reflect on viruses and the inflammatory response.
- Reflect on virus and antipyretic therapy in adults.

Scenario 12

New-born David is cared for at the neonatal intensive care unit. For more than 6 hours he has had a heart rate of more than 170 beats per minute and an unstable body temperature.

- Reflect on the innate and adaptive immune responses in neonates.
- Reflect on the function of the gut mucosal barrier.
- Reflect on pro-inflammatory cytokines.
- Reflect on lipopolysaccharides (LPS) and their pyrogenic effect.

Scenario 13

Mr. Smith, aged 75, is being cared for at the intensive care unit (ICU) because of septicaemia. He receives cooling blankets to treat the fever.

- Reflect on compensatory thermogenic mechanisms.
- Reflect on antipyretics.
- Reflect on fever phases and thermoregulation.

Scenario 14

Mrs. Devon is critically ill and being cared for at the neuro intensive care unit (NICU). She shivers several times a day.

- Reflect on cerebral injury and body temperature.
- Reflect on hyperthermia and acute-phase proteins response.

Scenario 15

Mr. Dean, aged 83, is on the second day of recovering from a hip replacement.

- Reflect on glucose and the inflammatory pathway.
- Reflect on the innate immune system.
- Reflect on thermoregulation and surgery.
- Reflect on the impact of age.

Scenario 16

Francis feels cold and has chills, Sally feels extremely weak, Nancy feels warm but is not sweating, Carl feels cold with gastro-intestinal symptoms, while Henry just feels under the weather and low. Two hours later they all have an increased body temperature assessed as fever.

- Reflect on the feelings of malaise.
- Reflect on fever phases.
- Reflect on cytokines and thermoregulation.
- Reflect on antipyretics.

Scenario 17

Cecilia has had fever and has not felt at all well for 3 days. At the primary health care centre her body temperature, measured in the ear, is assessed as normal.

- Reflect on the measuring technique and procedures.
- Reflect on standards.
- Reflect on the definition of fever.
- Reflect on your measurement reference.
- Reflect on calibration.
- Reflect on accuracy, stability and repeatability.
- Reflects on accuracy in clinical practice.

Scenario 18

Carl lives in a house in a Danish city. He goes out without his coat to get the newspaper on a cold, windy winter's morning. The wind slams the door behind him and Carl has no key. Standing outside the wind, his skin temperature drops quickly.

- Reflect on peripheral signals to the hypothalamus.
- Reflect on the stages of hypothermia.
- Reflect on the shivering response.
- Reflect on thermoregulation and metabolism.
- Reflect on a cold, rainy day.
- Reflect on a very hot day.

Index[1]

[1] Note: Page numbers followed by 'n' refer to notes.

E. Grodzinsky, M. Sund Levander (eds.), *Understanding Fever and Body Temperature*, https://doi.org/10.1007/978-3-030-21886-7

FSC
www.fsc.org
MIX
Papier | Fördert gute Waldnutzung
FSC® C083411

Kolibri 360 GmbH
Ferdinand-Jühlke-Straße 7
99095 Erfurt, Deutschland
produktsicherheit@kolibri360.de